CULTURE SMART!
PORTUGAL

Sandy Guedes de Queiroz

·K·U·P·E·R·A·R·D·

ISBN 978 1 85733 864 5
This book is also available as an e-book: eISBN 978 1 85733 865 2

British Library Cataloguing in Publication Data
A CIP catalogue entry for this book is available from the British Library

First published in Great Britain
by Kuperard, an imprint of Bravo Ltd
59 Hutton Grove, London N12 8DS
Tel: +44 (0) 20 8446 2440 Fax: +44 (0) 20 8446 2441
www.culturesmart.co.uk
Inquiries: sales@kuperard.co.uk

Series Editor Geoffrey Chesler
Design Bobby Birchall

Printed in Malaysia

About the Author

SANDY GUEDES DE QUEIROZ is a bicultural translator,
writer, editor, and relocation consultant. Educated in
London (UK) and Toronto, she earned her undergraduate
degree in Film & Communications from McGill University
in Montreal, and a postgraduate degree in Marketing from
Universidade Católica in Lisbon. A Portuguese native who
spent most of her childhood abroad and has lived in several
cities in North America and Portugal, Sandy currently lives
near Lisbon with her husband and three children.

The Culture Smart! series is continuing to expand.
For further information and latest titles visit
www.culturesmart.co.uk

The publishers would like to thank **CultureSmart!**Consulting for
its help in researching and developing the concept for this series.

CultureSmart!Consulting creates tailor-made seminars and
consultancy programs to meet a wide range of corporate,
public-sector, and individual needs. Whether delivering courses
on multicultural team building in the USA, preparing Chinese
engineers for a posting in Europe, training call-center staff in India,
or raising the awareness of police forces to the needs of diverse
ethnic communities, it provides essential, practical, and powerful
skills worldwide to an increasingly international workforce.

For details, visit www.culturesmartconsulting.com

CultureSmart!Consulting and **CultureSmart!** guides have both
contributed to and featured regularly in the weekly travel program
"Fast Track" on BBC World TV.

contents

Map of Portugal   7
Introduction   8
Key Facts   10

Chapter 1: LAND AND PEOPLE   12
• Geography   12
• Climate and Weather   14
• Regions   15
• A Brief History   21
• Government   42
• The Economy   43
• Portugal Today   45
• Portuguese: A World Culture   46

Chapter 2: VALUES AND ATTITUDES   48
• Family   48
• Sociability   51
• Suspicion and Acceptance   52
• Individualism Versus National Pride   52
• *Machismo*   54
• Tolerance and Prejudice   54
• Religion   56
• Formality and Respect   59
• *Saudade*   61

Chapter 3: CUSTOMS AND TRADITIONS   62
• *"Tipico"*   62
• Public Holidays   62
• Religious Holidays   63
• Carnival   66
• Popular Saints   67
• Family Celebrations   70
• *Fado*   72
• Ribbon-Burning   75
• Bullfighting   76

Chapter 4: MAKING FRIENDS 80
- Close-Knit Circles 80
- Invitations Home 82
- Gift Giving 82
- Sports Clubs 83
- Expatriate Clubs 83
- English-Language Publications 84

Chapter 5: THE PORTUGUESE AT HOME 86
- Portuguese Homes 86
- The Household 88
- Shopping 90
- Daily Life 92
- Television 96
- Children 96
- Education 98
- Bureaucracy 99
- Military Service 100

Chapter 6: TIME OUT 102
- Food 102
- Wine 109
- Eating Out 113
- Nightlife 114
- Shopping for Pleasure 115
- Banks 116
- Sports 118
- Vacations 121
- Cultural Activities 122

Chapter 7: TRAVEL, HEALTH AND SAFETY 124
- Entering the Country 124
- Flying 124
- Trains 125
- Buses 127
- Driving 128

contents

- Rules of the Road   131
- Urban Transportation   134
- Where to Stay   136
- Health   139
- Safety   139

Chapter 8: BUSINESS BRIEFING   **140**
- The Business Culture   140
- Labor   143
- Company Structure and Organization   144
- Contracts and Fulfillment   145
- Communication Style   146
- Presentations and Negotiations   148
- Teamwork   149
- Dress Code   150
- Business Entertaining   150
- Women in Business   151

Chapter 9: COMMUNICATING   **152**
- The Portuguese Language   152
- Getting By   154
- Face-to-Face   156
- Humor   158
- The Media   159
- Telephone   161
- Postal Services   162
- Conclusion   163

Useful Resources   **165**
Further Reading   **165**
Index   **166**
Acknowledgments   **168**

Map of Portugal

introduction

Legend has it that when Caesar's general arrived
on Portuguese soil in the first century CE, he
claimed to have discovered a lovely country
blessed with a mild climate and a beautiful
coastline, but whose inhabitants were
ungoverned and ungovernable. The Portuguese
are still impulsive, set in their ways, and resistant
to change, yet they are ever charming, romantic,
and nostalgic, with an unshakable loyalty toward
family and friends. Their national pride is easily
roused, and celebrations of their history and
heritage burst forth at every opportunity. This is,
after all, the nation of Vasco da Gama and Henry
the Navigator—whose daring explorers first
rounded the Cape of Good Hope, discovered
the maritime route to the Orient, and colonized
lands in South America, Africa, and Asia. *Culture
Smart! Portugal* reveals a country that, having
enjoyed periods of great power and influence,
and endured times of economic hardship and
political turmoil, is striving to regain prosperity
and respect from its neighbors and the rest of
the world.

Portugal is a land of contrasts and
contradictions. Opulence dwells side by side
with simplicity. Elegant homes nestle inside

old, seemingly decrepit buildings. Lush green
hills blend with jagged landscapes. The people
themselves are colorful, diverse, and multifaceted.
Take the time to get to know them, and you will
find them hardworking and eager to please.
Culture Smart! Portugal takes you beneath the
surface of this fascinating country and shows
you how to blend in and make the most of your
visit. In these pages, you will gain insight into
Portuguese priorities and values and learn how
to tap into a helpful and resourceful nature that
is often overlooked by the casual visitor.

In business and at home, the Portuguese are
self-deprecating, fatalistic, and individualistic, in
an unthreatening and even amusing way that can
be both frustrating and enchanting. Beneath
a rather vociferous manner, they are laid-back
and gentle. Tourists are welcomed with a certain
fascination and curiosity, and people from
countries considered "world powers" are regarded
as somehow smarter and more credible than
themselves. So slacken your pace, put away your
watch, and enjoy the rich meals, lively festivals,
and ancient traditions. Make yourself available,
and experience firsthand how guests in Portugal
are treated as privileged members of the family.

Key Facts

Official Name	República Portuguesa (Republic of Portugal)	Member of the European Union and NATO
Capital City	Lisboa (Lisbon)	
Main Cities	Porto, Coimbra, Faro	
Area	35,580 sq. miles (92,152 sq. km)	
Geography	Situated on the westernmost tip of Europe, bordered to the north and east by Spain, and to the south and west by the Atlantic	
Climate	Mild (Mediterranean)	
Currency	The Euro, since January 1999	Previously the Portuguese escudo
Population	10.4 million (2014)	
Ethnic Makeup	92.6% Portuguese	
National Language	Portuguese	Barranquenho is a dialect spoken only in the southern area of Barrancos, and Mirandês is a dialect used only on the northeastern border with Spain.
Religion	81% Roman Catholic	
Government	Democratic republic with the president as head of state and the prime minister as leader of government	Presidential elections are held every five years. Parliamentary elections are held every four years.

Media	The national public television networks are RTP1 and RTP2, and the main private networks are SIC and TVI, as well as a number of private sports and news channels. Cable and satellite television is readily available through 3 main providers (Vodafone, MEO, and NOS), offering a wide array of national and foreign channels. The public radio stations are Antena 1, 2,and 3. There are also numerous private stations.	The main daily newspapers are *Diário de Notícias* (Lisbon), *Jornal de Notícias* (Porto), and *Público*. The main weekend papers are *Expresso* and *Semanário*.
Media: English Language	The *Portugal News* and the *Resident*	
Electricity	220 volts, 50 Hz	Two-prong plugs are used. Transformers are required for US appliances.
Video/TV	PAL BG system	US video systems are not compatible.
Internet Domain	.pt	
Telephone	Portugal's country code is 351.	To dial out of Portugal, dial 00 followed by the country code.
Time	Greenwich Mean Time, five hours ahead of US Eastern Standard Time	

LAND & PEOPLE

GEOGRAPHY

Portuguese territory is divided between continental Portugal, at the westernmost tip of the Iberian Peninsula, and the archipelagos of the Azores and Madeira in the Atlantic Ocean. Continental Portugal shares borders with Spain to the north and east, while the western and southern extremities dive directly into the Atlantic.

On the continent, Portugal spans 349 miles (561 km) at its longest and 135 miles (218 km) at its widest, making it a small rectangle that can be quite easily covered in a short amount of time. The frontiers are partly defined by the four major rivers, the Minho and the Douro in the north, the Tagus (Tejo) and the Guadiana in the south. Elsewhere they are marked by mountain ranges.

The continental territory is divided into eighteen districts, with each district's capital city bearing that district's name. The districts from north to south are Viana do Castelo, Braga, Vila Real, Bragança, Porto, Aveiro, Viseu, Guarda, Coimbra, Leiria, Castelo Branco, Santarém, Portalegre, Lisbon, Setúbal, Évora, Beja, and Faro.

Madeira is situated 566 miles (910 km) southwest of Lisbon and is comprised of the islands of Madeira and Porto Santo, which make up the Funchal district. The Azores archipelago lies 769 miles (1,238 km) west of Lisbon and is formed by the Horta, Angra do Heroísmo, and Ponta Delgada districts, with a total of nine islands.

The capital, Lisbon, is situated on the coast more or less in the middle of the national territory, at the mouth of the Tagus River. Lisbon's history spans over twenty centuries, and this is still visible today.

Although Lisbon is a modern and cosmopolitan city, one can still relive the old classical traditions in the ancient neighborhoods of narrow cobblestone streets and medieval architecture where old houses still stand alongside ancient palaces and grand churches.

Following the coast north, to where the Douro River meets the Atlantic, is Porto. With a Unesco

World Heritage classification for its historic center and a dynamic business and cultural life, Porto is considered Portugal's second capital.

The differences that distinguish Lisbon and Porto could at first glance hint at a certain rivalry between the two cities, but they actually complement each other. Whereas Lisbon at first comes across as a very classical, traditional city, the people are more modern, cosmopolitan, and open-minded. Porto, on the other hand, is outwardly modern in terms of aesthetics and sense of style (architecture, art, décor, fashion), yet at heart its inhabitants are very traditional and home-loving.

CLIMATE AND WEATHER

Despite its relatively small expanse, continental Portugal's climate varies significantly from region to region, with pronounced differences in temperature between the north and the south as well as between the coast and the territories further inland. Generally, however, the climate is mild, with daily temperatures ranging between 46.4°F and 64.4°F (8°C and 18°C) in the winter and 60.8°F and 86°F (16°C and 30°C) in the summer.

As with almost everything to do with Portugal, the climate can be divided into north, center, and south. The north registers higher precipitation with more rain and lower temperatures, whereas south of the Tagus River, due to the Mediterranean influence, the winters are shorter and drier and the summers extremely hot. The climate in the center, of course, lies somewhere in between. It is inland in the mountainous regions, however, where the climate ranges between bitter cold and snow in the winter and a parched, overbearing heat in the summer.

The Madeira Islands boast a typically Mediterranean climate, with mild temperatures and conditions all year-round, whereas the Azores, while also mild, have a more bracing maritime climate and an abundance of rain.

REGIONS

Though culturally the Portuguese divide their country into north, center, and south, Portugal is divided into eight geographic regions, plus the Madeira and Azores archipelagos, which are, for administrative purposes, each considered "autonomous regions."

Entre Douro e Minho

The Minho and Douro Rivers give the northwestern region its name, Entre Douro e Minho. Translated

literally as "Between Douro and Minho," this
region includes the Viana do Castelo, Braga, Porto,
and northern Aveiro districts. Usually referred to
only as "Minho," the coastal area is flat, whereas
further inland it becomes hilly and mountainous.
The *Minhoto* culture is rich in tradition and
folklore that is most evident during the
local festivals.

Trás-os-Montes e Alto Douro
Directly East of Minho lies the Trás-os-Montes
e Alto Douro region, also shortened to simply
"Trás-os-Montes" for practicality. This region
encompasses Vila Real, Bragança, northern
Viseu, and northern Guarda. Its agriculture
consists mainly of almond trees and the vines
that produce grapes for the famous Port and
Douro wines. This region is rich in traditional
dialects that can make the locals quite difficult
to understand.

Beira Interior

South of Trás-os-Montes is the Beira Interior region, which is formed by southern Guarda and the Castelo Branco district. The summer here can be very hot, but in the winter this is where the coldest temperatures register, often dropping below zero with snow in the mountain ranges.

These regions comprise what is generally referred to as "the north." The inhabitants of this area often have to move to the larger cities for work, but are extremely attached to their hometowns and roots. People from the north are typically hot-blooded, quick-tempered, and very straightforward. They keep their relationships simple, expressing their thoughts and emotions in a rowdy and often harsh manner, but once an issue has been dealt with, they move on. The reigning philosophy is to forgive and forget, and their loyalty and friendship has no bounds—though they expect the same in return.

Beira Litoral

Next to Beira Interior, toward the coast, southern
Aveiro and Viseu, Coimbra, and parts of Leiria form
the Beira Litoral. The land here is flat by the coast
but becomes rocky inland. In this region industrial
activity abounds, but the area is renowned primarily
for its architectural beauty. Coimbra University was
the first in Portugal. Located in Lisbon at its inception
in 1290 and then relocated to its present site in 1537,
it is one of the oldest universities in Europe

Estremadura e Ribatejo

Between the Beiras and Lisbon lies the Estremadura
e Ribatejo region. This is an area where fertile soils,
watered by the Tagus River, produce an abundance
of fruit, vegetables, grain, tomatoes, olives, and
vines. Horse and bull breeding is also concentrated
here, and there are many enthusiastically attended
agricultural fairs and bullfights. This small, wealthy
region holds the country's highest concentration of

World Heritage sites, such as Alcobaça, Batalha, Fátima, and Mafra.

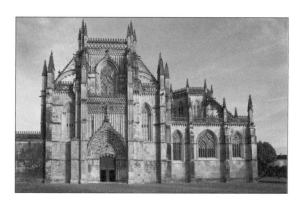

Lisboa e Setúbal

The Lisboa e Setúbal region is made up of those two districts. It is here that the rivers Tagus and Sado are found. This is one of the better-known regions and is a tourist attraction due to its pleasant climate, green countryside, and beautiful beaches.

The area known as "the center" lies roughly between Setúbal and Coimbra. Here the people have a more modern and cosmopolitan attitude that can make them come across as aloof and inaccessible in comparison to their northerly neighbors. Friendships may seem more superficial, but this is primarily due to a more reserved and temperate nature. Feelings are either kept hidden or expressed in a more diplomatic manner, though there is always the possibility that someone is holding a grudge.

Alentejo
The Alentejo region is the largest district and includes southern Setúbal, Beja, Évora, and Portalegre. The land is mostly flat and dry, due to low precipitation all year-round and an extreme heat in the summer that imbues its inhabitants with a sleepy, relaxed demeanor. Though this region dedicates itself mainly to farming, the coast is quite wild and beautiful and is becoming a growing tourist attraction. *Alentejanos* are a typically rural population who, living in large, extended family units, often miles away from the next household, generally keep to themselves. Life here revolves around the dining table, and as in the Ribatejo, local fairs are very popular.

Algarve
At the southernmost tip of Portugal lies the

Algarve, made up wholly of the Faro district. This is probably the best-known region, since it depends greatly on tourism. Due to a lack of rivers, this area is very dry and hot and boasts a Mediterranean climate.

The Alentejo and Algarve are what make up "the south," where a permanently procrastinating and laid-back attitude pervades. Away from the coast people often live on properties that may be miles from their closest neighbor or town, and this brings about a tendency to socialize little and keep to oneself. Foreigners and strangers are treated as just that and are usually kept at a comfortable distance. Closer to the coast and the more touristy areas, however, the inhabitants of the south are very much aware that their livelihood depends on visitors. Thus a concerted effort is made by all to communicate and be understood, and it is common to hear even the least cosmopolitan of locals speak some broken English or German.

A BRIEF HISTORY
Early Inhabitants

The Iberian Peninsula's location between the Atlantic Ocean, the Cantabrian Sea (the southern part of the Bay of Biscay), and the Mediterranean provides an easy link between the European and African continents. This, as well as the mild and pleasant climate, has made it especially attractive for passage and settlement by many peoples down the ages.

The earliest inhabitants to leave their mark were the races of the Neolithic culture, believed to have traveled to the Iberian Peninsula from

Minor between 3,000 and 4,000 BCE in search of minerals. Remnants of dolmens (large stone chamber tombs) produced by this culture can still be found in the Algarve and Andalusian Spain. The Phoenicians, who were traders and navigators, arrived around the twelfth century bce, followed by the Iberians. Though the Iberians, to whom the peninsula owes its name, are believed to have first migrated to the Ebro Valley from North Africa in the Iron Age, their presence in Portugal in historical records dates to around the sixth century BCE, settling after the Phoenicians.

Around the seventh century BCE the Greeks, also merchants, arrived, followed a century later by the Celts from central Europe. The Celts held an enormous advantage over the earlier inhabitants in that they were skilled ironworkers. Whereas previous settlers had come in search

of copper and tin to transform into bronze, iron could be used not only for adornments and arms but also to make farming tools; with crops growing and hunger diminishing, the population thrived. The Celts were also gifted goldsmiths and from them the Portuguese would inherit their craftsmanship and the traditional *Minhoto* (meaning "from Minho") filigree designs that are still created and worn today.

The Carthaginians, descendants of the Phoenicians, settled in the territory around the third century BCE, and dedicated themselves mainly to commerce and salting fish. The Romans expelled them that same century, during the Punic Wars. The fusion of these rich and diverse cultures—primarily between the Celts and the Iberians, who produced a race called the Celtiberians—created the people the Romans referred to as the Lusitanians. They were the tribe who occupied Lusitania, the lands that stretched between the Tagus and Douro Rivers. They were considered "the strongest of all the Iberian nations" and remained known throughout history for their courage and bravery. The word *Lusitano* is still used today to describe all things Portuguese.

The Romans

When the Romans invaded the Iberian Peninsula in 219 BCE, they found Celts north of the Douro River and Lusitanians between the Douro and Tagus Rivers. It was the Lusitanians, led by a humble but courageous shepherd named Viriato, who offered them the greatest resistance and whose name would become a symbol of Portuguese independence.

The Roman presence lasted approximately seven centuries. During this time they founded cities—Olispo (Lisbon), Bracara (Braga), Scalabis (Santarém)—and built roads, bridges, and

monuments, some of which still exist today. The founding of schools led to the spread of literacy and, from Latin, the local people under Roman influence created a dialect that would eventually become the Portuguese language.

Vandals and Visigoths

In the year 416 CE, while the Romans were fighting barbarian invasions on several fronts, the Suebi and the Vandals occupied the Iberian Peninsula. They in turn were pushed into the northwest and eventually conquered by the Visigoths. The Germanic kingdoms lasted for three centuries, adopting the existing Roman social, administrative, and economic structures. They also introduced laws concerning the ownership and inheritance of land, which led to a stratified society based on wealth and birth. Thus were cast the fundamental social divisions of clergy, nobility, and the people, a model that would later be adopted by medieval Portuguese society.

The Vandals and Visigoths subscribed to Arianism, a heretical form of Christianity, and persecuted the native Catholic Church. This complicated even further the fusion between the Germanic cultures and the Christian Hispano-Romans, until 589 CE, when King Reccared and all the Visigoths converted from Arianism to Catholicism. Thereafter the Christian kings of Spain, divinely appointed, worked closely with the Church to form an ideology of kingship.

The Moors

In the seventh century, the Arabs swept out of the Arabian Peninsula to spread the new religion of Islam by conquest. In 711 CE the Moors—Arabs and converted Berbers from North Africa—sailed across the narrow sea and overran the Iberian Peninsula. There they would remain for over five centuries. Apart from an undefeated Visigothic remnant in the inhospitable north, which formed the nucleus of resistance, Portugal and Spain were absorbed into the Umayyad Caliphate.

In the ninth century the Christian kingdoms of the northeast began a centuries-long counteroffensive known as the *reconquista*, and the Caliphate of Cordova, after a period of internal strife, eventually disintegrated into a number of independent kingdoms. The Christian advance was checked by the Moroccan Almoravids in the late eleventh and early twelfth centuries, and again in the 1150s by the sectarian Shi'ite Almohads.

By and large, Muslim rule was benign. The Moors produced a brilliant, multiethnic civilization in the Iberian Peninsula that stimulated the search for knowledge, allowed freedom of worship, and ushered in a period of cultural and intellectual cross-fertilization. Their treatment of their subject peoples depended on the attitude of those peoples toward the Islamic religion. If they converted, they were accepted into the community with equal rights and duties. If they maintained their Christian faith, they could own land and practice their religion, though with limitations, and were obliged to pay a tax. If they resisted with arms, they were either slaughtered or sold into slavery.

Moorish influence was greatest in the south and is still evident today in the whitewashed houses and rounded chimneys typical of the Algarve. The Moors also added new vocabulary to the existing Roman language, and brought about economic and technical renewal—for instance, by the use of the Alcatruz wheel to raise water from the riverbeds to channels for irrigation.

Kings and Kingdoms

The expansion of the Christian Kingdom of León in the twelfth century liberated much of Portugal. While the Almoravid caliphs were reestablishing Muslim control of the south, in the north Alfonso

VI, King of León and Castile, enlisted foreign nobles to his cause. To his aid came the cousins Raymond and Henry of Burgundy (Raimundo and Henrique de Bourgogne), descendants of Robert II, King of France. As a token of his thanks, Alfonso gave Raimundo his daughter Urraca's hand in marriage as well as the county of Galicia, and to Henrique he gave his daughter Teresa and the county of Portucale (Portugal), which stretched between the Minho and Tagus Rivers.

Henrique made Guimarães the capital of Portucale and ruled as a vassal of Alfonso, securing the Galician marches from Moorish raids. He held the firm desire to turn the county into an independent kingdom, but died in 1112 before seeing his dream realized. Upon his death, Teresa governed as regent, their son Afonso Henriques being only three years old. At the age of thirteen Afonso Henriques declared himself king and vowed to gain independence from León. In 1128 he seized control from his mother, who remained loyal to the Galician court, defeating her at the battle of São Mamede. For nine years he fought Alfonso VI of León, and in 1139, after a

A Love Story

Dom Pedro and Inês de Castro were Portugal's real-life Romeo and Juliet. Inês, a beautiful Spanish noblewoman became lady-in-waiting to Constance of Castile when the latter traveled to Lisbon in 1340 to marry Dom Pedro, the crown prince and heir to the Portuguese throne. Dom Pedro and Inês fell in love, and though Pedro's father, King Afonso IV, banished her from the court, their love affair continued. When Constance died in 1345, Dom Pedro settled with Inês in Coimbra, where she bore him four children. Afonso maintained his opposition to the relationship and, in his son's absence, had Inês murdered. Distraught with grief and anger, Dom Pedro led a rebellion against his father, and on his death, when he was crowned King in 1357, had his lover's assassins murdered and tore their hearts out with his bare hands.

This tragic and romantic story is a favorite among the Portuguese, and has been featured widely in classical Portuguese literature.

great victory over the Moors at Ourique, he was crowned Afonso I, first king of an independent Portugal. Finally, in 1143, through the Treaty of Zamora, Alfonso recognized Portugal as an independent kingdom.

Afonso Henriques became known as "the Conqueror" because his successful campaigns against the Moors expanded the kingdom to the south. After the battle of Ourique in 1139, he created a banner with five small blue shields representing the five Moorish kings he had defeated, and in each blue shield he placed five white dots representing the five wounds of Christ. This coat of arms remains at the center of the modern Portuguese flag. In 1147 Afonso captured Lisbon with the help of a Crusader fleet, and he later defeated the Moors twice at Santarém, in 1171 and 1184. He founded a chivalric order, the Order of Aviz, in about 1162.

Afonso's heirs continued to campaign against the Moors in the south until their final defeat in 1249 by Afonso III, when the Algarve was added to Portugal. Attempted incursions by the Marinid Sultanate of Morocco were decisively defeated by Afonso IV of Portugal and Alfonso XI of Castile in 1340.

Toward the end of the fourteenth century, Portugal was in crisis, having suffered greatly from the plague and finding itself at risk of losing independence to Castile once again. The conflict between the Christian monarchs of the Iberian Peninsula was further fueled by the Hundred Years' War between England and France. In the interregnum that followed the death in 1383 of Ferdinand I, last king of the House of Burgundy, John (Juan) of Castile claimed the Portuguese throne for himself and laid siege to Lisbon. The regent, Ferdinand's half-brother John (João), the Grand Master of Aviz, defeated the Spanish and was crowned king, as João I. Thus began the Aviz dynasty. Reinforced by English archers, João defeated the Castilians at the battle of Aljubarrota and ushered in a period of reform at home and discovery and expansion overseas. He made a treaty of friendship with England, and in 1387 married Philippa of Lancaster, daughter of John of Gaunt, so initiating Portugal's earliest alliance with Great Britain.

THE ALJUBARROTA BAKER

Brites de Almeida, a local baker, became a popular historical figure when, on August 14, 1385, she contributed to the Portuguese victory in the Battle of Aljubarrota. Brites discovered seven Castilians hidden in her oven. Legend has it that she killed all seven with her baker's paddle, and since then, the spade remains the town's banner.

The Age of Discovery and Exploration

It was João and Philippa's sons, Duarte, Pedro, and Henrique, who proposed discovering what lay beyond Cape Bojador on the Atlantic coast

of Africa, and the capture and conversion of the Moroccan city of Ceuta in 1415. Henrique, the famous Henry the Navigator, then settled in Sagres in the Algarve, where he founded a nautical school and surrounded himself with cartographers, astronomers, geographers, mathematicians, navigators, and shipbuilding specialists. From here, expeditions would set sail and Portugal would amass a vast commercial and colonial empire spread throughout Africa, Asia, and South America.

Thus, in 1419 the Portuguese discovered Madeira, in 1427 the Azores, in 1456 Cabo Verde and Guinea, and in 1471 São Tomé and Principe. João II, the "perfect prince," coordinated all known navigational knowledge, drawing on Arab and Jewish mathematical and astronomical sources, in what has been called the "first scientific revolution," so laying the foundations of European science a century later. Under João II's guidance the Portuguese continued to explore Africa's Atlantic coast, and in 1488 Bartholomeu Dias rounded the Cape of Torments at the southern point of Africa, which João renamed the "Cape of Good Hope." In July of 1497 Vasco da Gama set sail from Lisbon; less than a year later he anchored at India's great commercial port of Calicut. The maritime route to India had finally been discovered. In 1500 Pedro Alvares Cabral reached Brazil, and between 1519 and 1521 Fernão de Magalhães (Ferdinand Magellan) became the first mariner ever to circumnavigate the globe.

Losing and Restoring Independence
In the mid-1500s Portugal entered a period of decline. The expulsion, or forcible conversion, of the Jews in 1497 deprived it of its middle class and of its most talented traders and financiers. Large numbers settled in Holland, where they contributed greatly to the success of the rival Dutch commercial empire. The Holy Office, or

Inquisition, was established in Lisbon in 1536 to root out heresy.

In 1521, with the accession of John (João) III, the throne passed to the Habsburgs and came to be increasingly dominated by the Jesuits. The unworldly young king Sebastião launched a disastrously ill-prepared crusade against the Moors in Morocco that culminated in his death and the loss of the battle of Alcácer Quibir in 1578.

The vacuum created by this turn of events led to the invasion of Portugal by a Spanish army under the Duke of Alva, and in 1580 to the loss of independence to Philip II's Spain. Portugal was subject to the "Sixty Years' Captivity," during which time the country's finances, commerce, agriculture, and navy were ruined and the overseas empire abandoned. On December 1, 1640, a group of forty Portuguese noblemen, disgusted and frustrated with this neglect, stormed the viceroy's palace and the country united in the struggle to occupy forts and expel the Spanish troops. Two weeks later, João IV of the House of Braganza was proclaimed king.

The main goals following the restoration of independence were to keep foreign forces at bay, reorganize the country's economy, and attempt to regain some of the territories lost overseas. The Dutch were driven out of Brazil, and Portugal recovered its standing among European nations. Peace was finally settled between Spain and Portugal in 1668, and in 1703 the Methuen Treaty was signed with England, allowing Portugal to export wines to Britain and opening up the Portuguese market to English textiles. Also during this time, gold and diamonds were discovered in Brazil, filling the Portuguese coffers and funding many important works such as the building of Mafra's

convent and Lisbon's aqueduct, as well as libraries, academies, and museums.

The Lisbon Earthquake

On November 1—All Saints' Day—1755, a huge earthquake shook Lisbon, almost totally destroying the city, killing an estimated 20,000 people, and terrorizing the population. The scale of the disaster caused shockwaves throughout Europe, both actual and metaphorical, leading many thinking people to doubt the wisdom of divine providence and also to question social certainties. Others saw it as divine wrath, a terrible warning to sinners. The timid King José Manuel's clear-sighted and practical prime minister, Sebastião José de Carvalho, later made the Marquis of Pombal, took charge of the situation and rebuilt the capital as an elegantly planned modern city dedicated to commerce and industry. He set up

a government of technocrats, reduced the power of the Inquisition, expelled the Jesuits, introduced secular education, reorganized the county's finances, and promoted trade.

The Long Decline

In 1807 Napoleon's armies invaded Portugal and the court fled to Brazil. Portuguese forces fought the French from 1807 to 1811, and with England's help forced them to withdraw. The Anglo-Portuguese troops were led by Sir Arthur Wellesley (later the Duke of Wellington), who was given three important Portuguese titles as a sign of gratitude for his aid.

In the years that followed, Portugal suffered great internal turmoil. In 1820 the liberal revolution forced the king to return from Brazil and accept constitutional government. Brazil declared independence in 1822. In 1826 the Constitution was replaced with a more conservative document. In 1828, Queen Maria's accession was blocked by her uncle, Dom Miguel, who declared himself an absolute monarch. Civil war broke out between liberals and conservatives. In 1834 Queen Maria regained her throne with British, French, and Brazilian help, and constitutional government was restored. However, recurrent epidemics of cholera and yellow fever had begun, and would continue to decimate the population until the late 1850s. In the 1840s there were severe disputes between radicals and liberals. In 1851 the Duke of Saldanha staged a coup and launched a program of "regeneration" to promote order and economic growth. The late nineteenth century saw severe financial difficulties and the rise of socialist, anarchist, and republican parties.

In 1885 the Berlin Treaty, signed by the major imperial powers, stipulated that Africa should be shared among European nations, with Portugal taking control of the territories between Angola and Mozambique. In 1890, however, Great Britain gave Portugal an ultimatum, threatening to invade the Portuguese colonies if Portugal refused to remove its troops from the Chire valley, in

Chiromo, near Mozambique. Being at a military disadvantage, Portugal was forced to acquiesce. King Carlos I suspended the Constitution in 1907 and installed João Franco as dictator. Discontentment with Franco's measures led to the first attempt to install a republican regime. Carlos and his heir Luis Filipe were assassinated in the streets of Lisbon in 1908. Carlos's second son took the throne as Manuel II, but for only a short time. Two years later a republican revolution forced the royal family to flee to England.

The First Republic and the "Estado Novo"

On October 5, 1910, after a three-day insurrection, Portugal was proclaimed a republic. Although the new regime adopted a liberal Constitution in 1911, it involved several parties more interested in power than in progress, and the years that followed mark a period of economic hardship, corruption, and acute political instability. In 1916, Britain pressured Portugal into seizing around seventy German merchant ships seeking refuge in the Tagus, thus forcing Portuguese participation in the First World War on the Allied side in Africa to defend its colonies against Germany. The devastating impact of the war—inflation, food shortages, and the human toll in France—led to a coup in 1917

A PROCLAMAÇÃO DA REPUBLICA PORTUGUEZA

by Bernardino Sidónio Pais, who became the first republican dictator of the twentieth century. He was assassinated a year later, and the country was plunged into chaos. Finally, in 1926, seeing no end to the desperate situation, General Gomes da Costa led a military coup that established a dictatorship that was to last forty-eight years. In 1928, António de Oliviera Salazar became minister of finance. His reforms created economic stability, rebuilding the country's confidence, and renewing the world's respect for Portugal.

In 1933 Salazar was nominated president of the Ministers' Council, and the following year military rule ended. The authoritarian corporatist Estado Novo ("New State") he created initiated a period of national reconstruction, raising the value of

Portuguese currency abroad, rebuilding the navy, building roads, ports, schools, and hospitals, and reviving agriculture and industry. However, fearful of atheist Communism, Salazar resisted demands for democratic change at home and in the colonies and maintained order by means of an unrestrained secret police.

Thanks to Salazar, Portugal was spared involvement in the Second World War and went on to profit greatly from the export of raw materials, particularly tungsten, to both sides. In 1949 Portugal became a founding member of NATO. In 1961, however, the remaining Portuguese colonies in India—the cities of

Spy Stories

With Portugal being neutral during the Second World War, Lisbon was filled with spies. If you head west from the capital and follow the coast toward Cabo da Roca, the westernmost tip of Europe, you will pass Estoril, a lovely seaside town on a coastline that has often been compared with the French Riviera. Estoril's casino, the largest in Europe at the time, was a favored spot for spies to meet and exchange intelligence. This was so common and blatant that numerous authors, such as John le Carré and Graham Greene, as well as the film *The Russia House,* used Estoril as a setting for their spy stories.

Goa, Damão, and Diu—were occupied by Indian forces. That same year, insurgency in Angola, Mozambique, and Guinea-Bissau brought on a debilitating colonial war that would last over a decade.

The Peaceful Revolution

Incapacitated by a stroke, Salazar was relieved of his office in 1968 and was succeeded by Marcello Caetano. A former member of Salazar's cabinets, Caetano was a great admirer of his predecessor. Though he was successful in his social and economic reforms, Caetano's political strategies were heavily opposed. His more liberal colleagues, his opponents, and country people felt that he had failed to democratize Portugal sufficiently. Discontent was brewing beneath the surface, and on April 25, 1974, a group of captains and generals staged an uprising against the autocratic regime. What began as a coup quickly became a revolution. Political parties mushroomed. Exiles returned, political prisoners were released, and soldiers carried red carnations in the barrels of their guns. In May the junta handed over power to a fifteen-man provisional government. The colonial

war was immediately ended and Portugal conceded independence to all the remaining colonies (except Macao), which, like Brazil, chose to retain Portuguese as their official language.

Portugal has since made giant strides in overcoming the malaise—the legacy of the decline of empire and the political unrest of the nineteenth century—that previously kept it apart from other developed nations. Entry into the European Economic Community (now the European Union) in 1986 had a profound impact on its economic development. Since then, Portugal has joined the global economy and gained greater international exposure, resulting in growing supply and demand, investment, exports, and public spending. One of the eleven founding members of the single European currency, Portugal's adoption of the euro in 1999 further enhanced this growth by lowering the national debt, inflation, and interest rates.

GOVERNMENT

Today Portugal is a pluralistic democracy in which the legislature, executive, and judiciary are fully separate. The president is head of state, and also commander in chief of the armed forces. He represents the Portuguese Republic and guarantees national independence, state unity, and the proper conduct of the democratic institutions. The president is elected for a five-year term of office and can serve a maximum of two consecutive terms. Parliament

is a single-chamber assembly representative of all citizens. Portuguese citizens over the age of eighteen can participate in elections, whether they live in Portugal or abroad. In addition to its legislative function, parliament supervises enforcement of the Constitution and its laws and monitors the government and public administration. It consists of 230 deputies, elected by geographically defined constituencies for a four-year mandate. The government is made up of the prime minister, the ministers' council, and secretaries and subsecretaries of state. The president, based on the results of the parliamentary elections, nominates the prime minister, generally the leader of the party with the most votes.

THE ECONOMY

Despite a debilitating recession that lasted for over a decade, following the political unrest in the 1970s, Portugal experienced one of the highest rates of economic growth in Europe in the latter part of the twentieth century. The global economic turmoil of the years 2009 to 2014 wreaked havoc on the country ultimately resulting in a European bailout program and strict austerity measures. Since the beginning of 2015, Portugal has begun

an economic comeback, attracting international
investment and bringing record growth rates in
many sectors.

Traditionally agricultural, roughly half
of Portugal's territory and 12 percent of its
workforce is still dedicated to farming, with
olive oil, cork, and wine being some of the main
products. Despite this, Portuguese agriculture
yields less than 3 percent of the country's GDP,
one of the lowest rates in Western Europe.

While other European nations underwent
heavy industrialization throughout the nineteenth
century, Portugal lagged behind. Industrialization
occurred slowly and in spurts, encountering
heavy opposition by landowners and the
aristocracy and taking second place to colonial
affairs. Thus, in the early twentieth century,
over 80 percent of the population was still rural.
Industrial expansion occurred under Salazar

in the 1950s, and since then the economy has become progressively mixed. Nowadays, industry represents around 22 percent of the country's production, though some of the main products, namely textiles and footwear, are currently under serious threat from the Far East. Accession to the EU has attracted a healthy rate of foreign direct investment. Portugal has used these funds to develop a strong services sector, primarily in the areas of finance and telecommunications, which have come to make up over 75 percent of GDP. The investment in education and infrastructures has paid off, and many multinational corporations have chosen to establish their expertise and business services centers in Portugal. Less than a three-hour flight from most European capitals, with a good offer of qualified, multilingual professionals at comparatively low cost, as well as an appealing climate and culture, are assets that have put Portugal on the map among companies looking for an optimal location for their business services.

PORTUGAL TODAY

Since entry into the European Union, Portugal has been an active participant in global affairs. In 1991, it was the guest country invited to showcase at Europalia, the biannual fall arts festival that spans six cities in Belgium and attracts visitors from all over Europe. In 1994, Lisbon was nominated the

European Union's culture capital, and in 1998 the city hosted Expo '98, the last of these international expositions in the twentieth century, which received eleven million visitors from all over the world during its four-month run. In 2001 it was Porto's turn to be the European Capital of Culture, with Guimarães, yet another Portuguese city, receiving the same honor in 2012.

Portuguese politicians have also played an important role in global politics. In 1995, Diogo Freitas do Amaral, the Portuguese minister of foreign affairs, was elected president of the fiftieth General Assembly of the United Nations. In 2004, José Manuel Durão Barroso stepped down as Portugal's prime minister to accept the presidency of the European Union, and in 2005, former Prime Minister António Guterres was elected as the tenth United Nations High Commissioner for Refugees and was one the candidates to succeed Ban Ki-moon as Secretary General of the United Nations.

PORTUGUESE: A WORLD CULTURE

Portuguese culture has a strong literary heritage, with poets, playwrights, and novelists of genius who have earned admiration and recognition both at home and abroad. This great tradition spans the ballads and love songs of the early Middle Ages, the Chronicles of Fernão Lopes, the plays of Gil Vicente, father of the Portuguese theater and

outstanding contributor to the sixteenth-century
Iberian Renaissance, and Portugal's national
literary masterpiece, the epic poem *Os Lusiadas*
by Luis de Camões. Having made a significant
contribution to European culture in the past, the
Portuguese tradition continues. The nineteenth-
century novels of Eça de Queiroz and the early
twentieth-century poetry of Fernando Pessoa,
contemporary artists such as Paula Rego and Joana
Vasconcelos, the acclaimed architect Alvaro Siza
Vieira, acclaimed film director Manoel de Oliveira
and writers such as José Saramago (winner of
the Nobel Prize for Literature in 1998), Antonio
Lobo Antunes, and José Cardoso Pires continue to
command international respect in culture and the
arts. In 2009 a new museum, Casa das Histórias,
designed by Edouardo Souto de Moura, was
opened to showcase Rego's work.

VALUES &
ATTITUDES

Portuguese society is close-knit and relationship-based, with the family at its core. Whether at work or play, personal contact is key. The Portuguese work to live, rather than vice versa, and any excuse to socialize and have fun is welcome. Yet while their capacity for pleasure is boundless, they also revel in nostalgia and cultivate fatalism. Open and friendly once at ease, they can be suspicious and defensive if feeling insecure or on unfamiliar terrain. Once you become accustomed to these contradictions, you will find them to be warm, outgoing people who are always ready for fun and celebration.

FAMILY

In the not-so-distant past it was common for traditional Portuguese families to be quite large, often having five or six children. As in the rest of Europe, however, over the last few decades Portugal has experienced a decline in its marriage and birth rates. Statistically, the average Portuguese family consists of 2.6 members, with 1.28 children to each woman, yet the concept of family has changed little.

Though a typical modern Portuguese home may consist of two parents and often only one child, the idea of the extended family is still very much alive. When a person refers to their family, they are not only considering their parents and siblings, but are also including a colorful array of grandparents, godparents, aunts, uncles, and cousins. Though this panoply of relatives does not necessarily reside under the same roof, family members generally live as close together as possible and maintain daily contact.

The decline in the number of offspring per family can be explained by several factors. Until the early 1960s, women made up 20 percent of the working population, the accepted norm being that they should marry young and stay at home bearing and rearing children. Since then, female university attendance has risen to 63 percent, and women now not only represent almost half the national workforce, but run 28.5 percent of companies in Portugal. One of the reasons this has been possible is thanks to the institution of "the grandparents." Since day care, public or private, is not an option for many families, grandparents are relied on to help with child care. Thus the elderly are both visible and respected, taking an active role in family life.

Some things have not changed, however. Mother definitely still rules the roost! At home it is still the wife who makes the domestic decisions and takes care of most of the domestic chores and duties, though this tendency is changing among younger couples. Another aspect that has stayed the same is that children live at home until they marry. Currently 55 percent of young people between the ages of eighteen and twenty-nine still live at home, and though 50 percent of those are employed, they are not expected to contribute to the family expenses. They do eventually end up flying the nest in their late-twenties, but while Portugal historically had one of the highest marriage rates in the European Union, in 2010 the rate began to drop and, at the moment, the country figures among the EU countries with the lowest marriage rate. This is due to a number of factors. On the one hand, youth unemployment was as high as 40.7 percent at the peak of the economic crisis, which severely compromised the young population's capacity to support themselves. On the other, as the older generations are replaced by younger people, religious practice has also diminished, and living with a partner outside of wedlock is becoming more accepted and commonplace.

Children are considered the center of the household. Not infrequently the mother works provoking a parental need to compensate the youngster in some form or another. Parents often go without in order to provide their children with luxuries, with the effect that children can often end up somewhat spoiled and overprotected. It is uncommon to see these children in public without adult supervision since they are almost always accompanied to and from school or when playing outside, even when older.

Being accustomed to adult company, children are usually sociable and confident and are often proudly paraded by their caretakers whenever possible.

Portuguese families value loyalty and discretion above all, and it is unacceptable to "air one's dirty laundry." Such large extended families, when reunited, can reach twenty or thirty individuals, and so it is natural that the occasional disagreement can arise. The Portuguese keep their personal issues to themselves and prefer to resolve them privately "*em família*" rather than make them public. If they do "*desabafar*" (get it off their chest), however, this is done in strict confidence, and it carries the implicit understanding that only family members are allowed to speak ill of the family.

SOCIABILITY

The Portuguese are at heart a sociable and friendly culture. First and foremost comes family, then friends. Friendships tend to be strong, usually lifelong and they are treated as family. Since the Portuguese love to socialize (at the local café, at work, at clubs), acquaintances are numerous and are also treated warmly, but these relationships are kept on a more superficial level, with the various social circles usually kept separate. The Portuguese are curious and eager to please, however, and when interest is shown toward someone, it is genuine. Be open and communicative and they will make it their personal mission to ensure you enjoy yourself.

SUSPICION AND ACCEPTANCE

The Portuguese need to place people within a social context in order to accept them and tend to be suspicious of strangers. Though they may seem unfriendly at first, in many cases going to the same grocer or having a mutual acquaintance or children the same age is enough to overcome their reserve. Foreigners, due to obvious differences in physical appearance or customs, are placed in a different framework that keeps them at bay, yet at the same time gives them the benefit of the doubt should they make an unfortunate gaffe. However, the quicker you adopt a "when in Rome" attitude and establish common ground, the sooner you will benefit from the fun and warmth of being accepted as an equal.

Since the Portuguese are very proud of their food, eating their dishes with enthusiasm is guaranteed to impress. Refrain from making a face if you see them eating whole small fish with their fingers or avidly sucking shrimp heads! Instead, try one yourself—you may be surprised. The Portuguese are very affectionate toward children, so a playful or tender gesture toward someone's child is sure to break down the parent's guard. Also, if you can be helpful in any way, this will warm people to you. For example, you could offer to carry your elderly neighbor's shopping bags home for her.

INDIVIDUALISM VERSUS NATIONAL PRIDE

Due to periods of political confusion and disruption throughout their history, and possibly as a form of self-preservation, the Portuguese have cultivated a certain individualism and fatalism. This has unfortunately led to a cynical and self-deprecating attitude as well as a lack of community spirit. The Portuguese love to speak harshly of their own country, but will act only to better their own situation rather than attempt to improve the common good. Just as in family matters, while it is acceptable for the Portuguese to criticize their own country, it is not acceptable for an outsider to do so.

Underlying the Portuguese people's frustration is a strong sense of pride in their country's accomplishments and in their region's customs and traditions. Of course, what most fills the Portuguese with national pride is soccer. When Portugal defeated France in the final of the Euro 2016 Championship, and despite the absence of their captain Cristiano Ronaldo, who was injured and carried off the pitch in the first 25 minutes of the match, the morale of the country sky-rocketed. The victory party, set off with blasts of red and green water cannons to welcome home the heroes, lasted for weeks.

MACHISMO

Portuguese society seems at first glance male-dominated, but the underlying structure is definitely matriarchal. Though the men are hot-blooded Latinos at heart who love to size up and discuss the attributes of women in general, "their" women (mothers, sisters, wives, daughters, girlfriends) are completely off-limits. Men definitely behave differently when they are among themselves than when they are with female company. This of course is changing as society becomes more equal and better integrated, and has both positive and negative aspects. On the one hand, most men treat women like ladies, politely opening doors, pulling out chairs for them, refraining from crude language, and generally behaving with decorum. On the other hand, when on their own, they can adopt loud and vulgar language and engage in whistling and catcalling. This behavior, though provocative, is generally harmless and best ignored. Portuguese men also display aggressive expressions of *machismo* when blowing off steam—or when behind the wheel (see Chapter 6).

TOLERANCE AND PREJUDICE

The Portuguese consider themselves tolerant, but are not concerned with being politically correct. They are direct and speak their minds, sometimes regardless of whether what they say can be considered offensive, and are annoyed by people who beat around the bush and sugarcoat their opinions. Nonetheless, their exposure to different cultures, politics, and races is somewhat limited, so if a derogatory remark is made, it is usually due to ignorance rather than a mean or hurtful intent.

As colonizers went, the Portuguese were considered among the fairest and inclusive, and began emancipating slaves in Portugal in 1761, well before other nations did the same. Immigrants from ex-colonies are for the most part people with very little education who had suffered personal and economic hardship in their own countries and moved to Portugal searching for work and a better life. One must bear in mind that these are the references the Portuguese use when forming their opinions regarding people of different color.

Sexual tolerance has become more widespread as generations change and the country is more exposed to different realities through tourism and trade. In 2010, Portugal became the eighth country in the world to approve gay marriage and, in 2016, a bill legalising adoption was by same-sex couples was also passed.

Nevertheless there is a level of hypocrisy in certain Portuguese attitudes. If there is an accident involving personal injury or a fight breaks out in public, everyone will run to have a look. They have a very prudish outlook regarding sex, violence, and nudity, but explicit examples of these are found all over the television and media. Though there are some nude beaches, public nudity is generally not appreciated. Many female tourists choose to go topless, and though this is not necessarily condemned, most locals refrain from doing so themselves. Unless attending a nude beach, be modest, and do not change into or out of your bathing suit in public.

RELIGION

Portugal is still a religious country. "*Se Deus quiser*," translated as "God willing," is one of the most common endings to a Portuguese sentence. Eighty-one percent of the Portuguese population is Roman Catholic, with 19 percent attending mass regularly. Although this is proof that religion is very much a part of people's lives, however

 compared with the statistics ten years ago when 95 percent of the population was Roman Catholic and 50 percent attended mass at least once a month, there has been a clear decline in religious

affiliation. Nonetheless, even those who only go to church for social events such as weddings, baptisms, funerals, and religious holidays will prepare themselves scrupulously and attend with enthusiasm. This, of course, is in the spirit of family unity, and any excuse for a reunion is valid!

Though Catholicism is the dominant religion, the recent rise in immigration has brought about a cultural, ethnic, and religious diversity in which the Catholic Church now coexists peacefully with other religions.

The Miracle of the Roses

Isabel of Aragon (1269–1336), wife of King Dinis, was dubbed the Holy Queen and canonized in 1625 for the many miracles she performed. She was renowned for founding charities and hospitals, as well as visiting the poor and handing out coins and bread. The legend for which she is best remembered, the miracle of the roses, took place when she was concealing in her cloak a considerable amount of coins to give to the poor. This was an expensive practice of which the King did not approve. One day he intercepted her and asked her what she was carrying. When she opened her cape to show him, the coins had been transformed into roses, and so she simply replied, "Roses, my lord."

Fátima

The shrine of Fátima, near Leiria, is the religious heart of Portugal, drawing pilgrims from around the world throughout the year, who come to pray, give thanks, and strengthen their spiritual bond.

The story of the miracle of Fátima describes how, over a six-month period in 1917, the Virgin

Mary appeared to three young shepherds in Fátima and made three prophecies. The first was the confirmation of the existence of Hell; the second was the end of the First World War, with Russia's abandoning of the Christian faith and embracing of Communism, leading to war and persecution; and the third predicted an assassination attempt on Pope John Paul II.

After thirteen years of examination by clergy and scientists, in 1930 the Catholic Church pronounced the apparitions worthy of belief and the cult of Our Lady of Fátima was officially sanctioned.

Fátima's shrine and its symbolism are now so strong that even though many people today are no longer aware of the original story of the miracles, its spiritual significance is great enough to attract multitudes of worshipers year after year.

FORMALITY AND RESPECT

Manners and etiquette in Portugal are considered a sign of respect and are therefore highly regarded. That said, the Portuguese are quite lenient in this department as long as it is clear there is no disrespect intended. Foreigners are given the benefit of the doubt for being unfamiliar with local conduct, but if certain standards are practiced, your hosts will feel more comfortable and likely to accept you.

As a greeting in Portugal, women kiss men and each other on one or both cheeks. Men shake hands and the closer friends they are or the happier they are to see each other, the more vigorous the handshake, often accompanied by a bear hug and loud slaps on the back. In parting, the same ritual is repeated though the hugs and back pats are usually softer by this point.

The generation gap is reflected in peoples' behavior. Senior citizens still observe the old courtesies, and it is not uncommon to see an elderly man tip his hat in a lady's presence, or a gentleman greet an older lady by kissing her hand. From an early age, children are taught to treat adults respectfully. Hats are not worn indoors, youngsters are expected to stand up and greet elders when they enter a room, doing so again on parting, and so on. Though in theory adults and the elderly expect young people to behave appropriately, children's company is welcome and the attitude toward them is playful and permissive.

One example of the Portuguese affinity for formality and tradition is when a young couple decides to marry. Marriage in Portugal is not only the joining of two people, but is also expected to be the beginning of a lasting union between the bride's and groom's families. As a sign of respect, the groom may ask the bride's father for his daughter's hand in marriage. If choosing to abide by the more old-fashioned customs, he may meet with his future father-in-law in private and state his intentions. Or the young couple merely announce their decision and ask for their parents' blessing.

Once practical details regarding the wedding are decided upon and preparations are under way, a formal engagement celebration takes place, usually a few months before the marriage. This occasion is called the *pedido*, or proposal, and generally involves the bride's family inviting the groom's family for a meal. Here, the bride's father may make a speech welcoming the groom and his family into his household, followed by the groom who is also expected to address his future in-laws as well as formally propose to his bride and offer her an engagement ring. The *pedido* not only serves to make the engagement official, but also gives the families a chance to break the ice and get acquainted before the wedding day.

SAUDADE

The Portuguese are a nostalgic people. They are as nostalgic for what used to be as they are for what could have been, and this bittersweet, romantic fatalism is what is implied by the term "*saudade*." Portuguese elders love to sigh and lament and dwell on woeful stories, yet at the same time they have a great capacity for pleasure. This is yet another example of the colorful and contradictory nature of a people who love to mourn their plight, yet have a perpetual sense of fun and enjoy boisterous celebrations at national, religious, and family occasions.

chapter three

CUSTOMS & TRADITIONS

"*TÍPICO*"

The word "*típico*" is widely used and highly regarded in the Portuguese language. Translated literally as "typical," *típico* means anything traditionally, truly, typically Portuguese. There is typical everything: dishes, restaurants, customs, costumes, songs, dances… and these can vary from region to region or even town to town. These traditions have been cherished and maintained throughout the country's history and are proudly displayed during holidays and local festivals as an integral part of Portuguese culture.

PUBLIC HOLIDAYS

Portugal has fourteen public holidays throughout the year plus over a hundred municipal holidays. The national holidays celebrate either a religious or historical event, while the municipal celebrations usually honor the town's patron saint, with one day taken off work and local festivities that can last a week or more. When a holiday's date falls on a Thursday or Tuesday, it is common to take the Friday or Monday off ("*fazer ponte*"— "make a bridge") and extend the holiday to form a long weekend.

RELIGIOUS HOLIDAYS
Christmas and Easter are the most important religious holidays. Extended families use the occasion to get together, going to mass and sharing lavish meals of traditional food and plenty of wine.

Midnight mass (*missa do galo*) is attended on Christmas Eve (unofficially also a holiday, except

January 1	New Year's Day
February (always a Tuesday)	Carnival
March/April	Good Friday
March/April	Easter Sunday
April 25	Liberation Day
May 1	Labor Day
May/June	Corpus Christi
June 10	Portuguese National Day
August 15	Assumption Day
October 5	Proclamation of the Republic
November 1	All Saints Day
December 1	Restoration of Independence
December 8	Immaculate Conception
December 25	Christmas

for retail businesses), usually followed by a *ceia* or evening meal. On December 25 the festivities continue with lunch and often dinner as well. The menus vary from region to region, but Christmas meals are typically comprised of cod-based dishes as well as the traditional roast turkey, with rich desserts and pastries heavy in butter and sugary egg yolks. It is normal for families to travel around a lot during these two days in an attempt to see as many relatives as possible, and gifts are exchanged at each meeting. At this time of year, town and city centers are filled with lights, nativity scenes, and other traditional Christmas decorations. Most homes have a Christmas tree and nativity scene (*Presépio*) with Joseph, Mary, and Jesus in

the manger, as well as figurines of shepherds, animals, and the three wise men. The more modern figure of Santa Claus has permeated the once strictly religious holiday and is also included in the public and private decorations and festivities.

Palm Sunday, one week before Easter Sunday, marks the beginning of Holy Week (*Semana Santa*). Customs vary from town to town and region to region, the older neighborhoods and rural areas being more "typical" and maintaining the more traditional ceremonies, but the principal rituals are upheld throughout the country. On Palm Sunday, the last day of Lent, each parish holds a procession celebrating Christ's entry into Jerusalem. Often the priest takes the opportunity to visit parish homes and families, and it is customary for children to give their godparents flowers. Throughout the week, a variety of processions are carried out parading statues of Jesus and Mary, and people hang their most elaborate and treasured embroidered blankets and cloaks outside their windows and balconies.

Good Friday, the anniversary of Christ's crucifixion, is a day of fasting and spiritual reflection. There are also local processions and plays that reenact the Passion of Christ. On Easter

Sunday, churches are full and a general sense of celebration pervades. As is the case at Christmas, families unite for large, elaborate meals, and the international customs of offering and hunting for chocolate Easter eggs and rabbits are also practiced.

CARNIVAL

Carnival, or *Entrudo*, falls on the Tuesday before Ash Wednesday and marks the last day before Lent. Though not an official holiday, schools close on Carnival Monday and Tuesday, and many companies give their employees the day off. The Portuguese celebration of Carnival varies greatly throughout the country. Some cities, such as Loulé, choose to copy the Brazilian concept of carnival, with street dances and samba school competitions, while others prefer

putting local craftsmanship on display. In some areas, celebrations are of a more ceremonial and conservative nature, whereas in cities like Ovar or Torres Vedras, participants run loose, tickling and teasing onlookers or parading giant puppets that satirize historical figures and modern-day politicians. Generally, people use *Entrudo* as an excuse to dress up and have fun, be it publicly or privately, while others simply take the opportunity to get away and enjoy a long weekend.

POPULAR SAINTS

The month of June brings what is known as the Santos Populares, festivities of pagan origin celebrating the Summer Solstice. The favorite saints are Santo António (Saint Anthony), São João (Saint John), and São Pedro (Saint Peter), and though the reason these holy figures are associated with the summer folly is unknown, they have come to symbolize the connection between the sacred and the pagan. Between June and August, private and public balconies and patios all over the country are decked with lights, streamers, wild leeks, and potted basil. Communities come together to consume large quantities of grilled sardines, *caldo verde* (a traditional green cabbage soup), and wine in order to celebrate summer and ask the saints for good luck. The day following the celebrations is a municipal holiday.

Santo António

Santo António was an exemplary Franciscan
monk who was considered among other things
to be the protector of the poor and of single girls,
and a curer of infertility, the last two attributes
endowing him with matchmaking qualities.
Though not officially Lisbon's patron saint, he
has been "adopted" by the city, and the festivities
that honor him begin on June 12 with the Santo

António weddings.
Since 1950, the
city of Lisbon has
selected a group
from among
the city's poorer
engaged couples
to participate in a
public wedding.
After the ceremony,
the couples are
paraded around
the city, stopping at
the saint's statue to
offer him the bride's
bouquet before continuing on to the reception,
also provided by the city.

Also taking place that night are Lisbon's
"*Marchas Populares*." Avenida da Liberdade, one
of downtown Lisbon's main avenues, sets the
stage for a parade where over twenty associations
representing the traditional neighborhoods

compete in songs, choreography, and costumes. Each procession is an explosion of color and music that attempts to capture the essence of local tradition.

São João

In the north, the preferred saint is São João. As in the rest of the country, outdoor fairs and parties are organized where plenty of traditional singing and dancing takes place, with the night of São João being celebrated on June 23. In Porto, revelers roam the streets and squares armed with plastic hammers and wild leeks, banging them on the heads of passersby for good luck. It is best to maintain a sense of humor and take this behavior in the spirit of excess and good fun! Aside from the neighborhoods competing with their displays

of fireworks, it is also customary on this night for everyone to set large, colorful paper balloons alight and release them into the sky, watching them float, glowing, over the city.

FAMILY CELEBRATIONS

In the urban centers today family occasions are celebrated or marked in much the same way as in other cultures with Christian practices. Weddings, baptisms, and funerals in Portugal's small, rural communities, however, follow time-honored traditions.

Weddings

In traditional Portuguese weddings, the bridal party, consisting of the bride's extended family and close circle of friends, will go to the bride's home for breakfast and then accompany her to the church for the wedding ceremony, while the same occurs at the groom's family home. After the ceremony, the guests are invited to a reception where a lunch consisting of numerous courses and large quantities of wine and other beverages is served. Following lunch and dancing, it is customary for everyone to visit the newlyweds' home and then go home themselves for a siesta before meeting up again for another meal, usually but not necessarily lighter than the lunch. Sometimes guests are invited back the following day for leftovers! Wedding guests are expected to give the newlyweds a gift. In some cases

the bride and groom may have gift registries in shops where people can purchase items they have chosen beforehand, while in others, an envelope is passed around during the reception for guests to give money.

Baptisms
Because baptism is a child's introduction into the religious community, it is usually performed within the community at regular Sunday mass. Thus it is not uncommon during mass for there to be a number of babies (ranging from two or three to ten) waiting to be christened after the regular service. Baptisms are a smaller affair than weddings, usually restricted to family and close friends, but also involve a large meal afterward. It is also customary to take a gift for the child, usually a piece of silverwork with

religious significance, such as a cross pendant or a medallion portraying a saint.

Funerals
Funerals are solemn affairs that do not involve eating or drinking. A death is usually announced by the family in a local newspaper, along with the time and place of the funeral service for those wishing to pay their respects and attend services. People who want to offer their condolences may do so at the wake before the religious ceremony, and many churches and chapels place an attendance book in the entrance for those wishing to sign, as well as a plate to leave personal cards. Once the service has ended, attendants will follow the casket on foot (if a short distance) or drive to the cemetery for the burial, after which people go their separate ways. Women wear black or white for funerals, while men wear suits and a black tie. One week after the death, a seventh-day mass is held to pray for the deceased and for people once again to offer their condolences and pay their respects.

FADO
The precise origins of *fado* are unclear, but on one point everyone agrees: these quintessentially Portuguese melodies are the true expression of the Portuguese soul. The word "*fado*" derives from the Latin "*fatum*," which means fate. The

songs, melancholic lamentations accompanied by the Portuguese guitar, mirror the Portuguese romantic and fatalistic side, describing the pain and *saudade* of surrendering to one's destiny.

One theory states that *fado* descends from Moorish chants, which were also melancholic and doleful. Others suggest that the songs came from the medieval jesters and troubadours who sang about friendship and love as well as criticizing politics and society through satire. The most common explanation, however, is that *fado* derives from "*lundum*," the music sung by Brazilian slaves, and was brought to Lisbon in the mid-nineteenth century by Portuguese sailors. The first known *fado* songs speak of the sea and distant lands and therefore seem to support this theory.

The Portuguese guitar is one of *fado*'s main symbols, the other being the black shawl. Men usually sing *fado* wearing a dark suit, while women are also dressed in dark colors with a black shawl draped over one or both shoulders. Themes usually revolve around the pain of love and/or death, though individual songs can broach any subject from horses and bullfights to politics and patriotism. "Typical" *fado* is sung in small, dark restaurants and taverns in the older parts of Lisbon such as Alfama and the Bairro Alto, and the artists can be the most unlikely people, even one of the waiters serving tables. Though conversation can flow normally

when no one is performing, it is important to keep quiet when someone is singing or the singer and fellow patrons may take offense. Of course, with artists like Amália Rodrigues, Dulce Pontes, and Marisa, *fado* has reached an international audience and, thanks to the recordings of new artists like Carminho and Ana Moura, can also be enjoyed at home or in a more modern setting.

In Coimbra, the *fado* tradition took a slightly different direction. Coimbra housed the country's first university, and young people from Lisbon and Porto would flock there to receive their education, taking along their guitars and their songs and instilling *fado* in the student community. Little could better impress a young woman than a suitor standing under her window at night serenading her with heart-wrenching songs of unrequited love. Nor could any other music better explain the *saudade* of leaving behind the best years of one's youth and the bohemian student life. Thus *fado* became the official anthem for graduating university students. Toward the end of the academic year, groups of students from universities around the country can still be seen wandering the city streets at night in their thick black cloaks, playing their guitars and singing their serenades.

RIBBON-BURNING

The ribbon-burning (*queima das fitas*) tradition carried out by graduating university students, mainly in the north of Portugal, dates back to the mid-nineteenth century. Upon finishing their exams, students would group together by faculty and form a procession from the university to the town or city's main square, where they would burn the ribbons used to tie their books together. Over the years, this tradition has grown in participation and sophistication, and there is now an official ribbon-burning week in May, with organized activities and festivities.

This week usually begins with a monumental serenade where the academic community comes together to sing *fado* and other songs. At these concerts, rather than clapping, the students shake their satchels, displaying all their ribbons, which are covered with signatures of professors, colleagues, friends, and family. There is also usually a religious ceremony where

the ribbons and satchels are blessed. After this, the week continues with sketches that parody the professors and academic life, processions, and large parties and concerts. In Porto and Coimbra, ribbon-burning week is a major event, with the activities and events usually making the front pages of the newspapers.

BULLFIGHTING

Unlike in Spain, in Portugal the bull is not killed in the ring. At the end of the spectacle it is led out by a herd of cows to be slaughtered for beef.

Drawings found in caves throughout the Iberian Peninsula suggest that the ritualistic relationship between man and bull dates back to prehistory. The practice of letting bulls loose among crowds for amusement began during

the summer fairs and festivals of the Middle Ages. The art of bullfighting on horseback as it is seen today was developed as entertainment for the aristocracy in the sixteenth century. Later came the practice of bullfighting on foot, which brought the tradition to the masses. Bullfighting in Portugal is of extreme cultural importance; the Portuguese pride themselves on the rituals and traditions of what is considered an art form, and the *toureiros* (bullfighters) are regarded as heroes for their skill and bravery.

Bullfighting season begins on Easter Sunday and runs through to October. There are *corridas* (races) or *toiradas* (bullfights) throughout the country on most weekends, every Thursday night in Lisbon during the summer months, and every day during the weeklong rural fairs that take place in the Ribatejo. The Ribatejo is the

region northeast of Lisbon where the bullfighting tradition is strongest and where most of the bulls are bred. In each *corrida,* six or eight bulls are fought one at a time, with approximately half an hour allocated to each bull. The number of bullfighters varies between one and four, with each bullfighter usually facing two or three bulls. The *toureiro* performs either on horseback or on foot, never doing both. The *toiradas* themselves can be only on foot, only on horseback, or a variation of the two.

Bullfights follow a rigid set of rules and the fighters themselves are very superstitious, each with their own personal rituals for preparing for the fight. Once in the ring, the first part of the spectacle involves bullfighters on horseback dominating the bull with lances, while the matadors on foot show their skill leading the bull with a crimson cloak. For *corridas* on foot, the next phase is for the *banderilheiros* to face the bull head-on and stick pairs of small spears in its back, ending once again with the matador and his dance with the red cape. With *toiradas* on horseback, the show is brought to a close with the *pega*, where a group of eight *forcados* literally take the bull by the horns and tail and bring it to a standstill with their bare hands. A band plays *paso dobles* and other traditional bullfighting music to accompany the performance, and there is a trumpeter, who stands and plays certain notes to signal changes in the program. Bullfights are not for the squeamish, but observing the enthusiasm and appreciation shown by the crowd as they applaud, throw flowers, handkerchiefs, and even items of clothing is amusing and exciting entertainment in itself.

MAKING FRIENDS

With friendship being such a closed and family-oriented affair, it is possible for the visitor at first to find the Portuguese aloof and standoffish. They are wary of the unfamiliar, be it people or situations, and strangers are often greeted with a certain amount of reservation, but don't let this put you off. Once you have learned to respect the boundaries and principles outlined here, and have been accepted into their circle, you will find your efforts rewarded, and that you have made firm, loyal friendships that last a lifetime.

CLOSE-KNIT CIRCLES

Because they tend to keep company mostly with family or close friends they have known since childhood or adolescence, the Portuguese can seem suspicious of strangers. Once the ice is broken, however, and they feel assured there is no hidden agenda, they become affectionate and helpful, so if properly approached are easily won over.

Friendships in Portugal are nurtured and cherished, and maintaining regular contact is of utmost importance since it indicates you are willing to make an effort. When talking to someone, whether in person or on the phone, it is important to begin by inquiring about their and their family's general well-being before broaching the subject at hand. Asking about their health is always a good start since the Portuguese love describing symptoms, ailments, and medical consultations and diagnostics in great detail to anyone willing to listen.

Portuguese communities are small, independent worlds. Everyone knows everyone, and having a friend or acquaintance in common makes it easier to place and accept you. If you want to meet local people, use the neighborhood shops and become a regular in local cafés and taverns, so that people will begin to recognize and acknowledge you. It is likely that you will feel observed and talked about at first, but don't feel uncomfortable. The Portuguese do this openly without disguising the fact that they are making comments about someone in their presence. If you maintain an open and friendly demeanor, their assessment of you will be positive. Offering to help with anything they may require from you is also a sure way of being accepted. Don't forget, manners are highly regarded and until a certain level of intimacy is reached, as a sign of respect, people treat each other with some formality.

INVITATIONS HOME

The Portuguese love to entertain at home. If they think someone is on their own, they are quick to extend an invitation. They are proud of their local and family traditions and are eager to share these and impress guests with their heritage, so be sure to try the food offered, even if it seems unappetizing, since chances are it is a family recipe or something *típico*. It is important to your hosts that you feel welcome and comfortable so there is no need to be overly formal, though it is courteous to dress in a manner that is casual yet groomed. Bear in mind that although invitations are made out of genuine friendship and empathy, it is generally expected that the gesture will be reciprocated. Be sure to phone within the following few days to say thank you; this indicates not only gratitude for the courtesy offered but also a willingness to maintain contact.

GIFT GIVING

When visiting someone's home, be sure to greet everyone in the household, and on the first visit it is customary to offer the hostess a gift of red wine, chocolate, pastries, or flowers. Do not give carnations as these carry a political meaning: red carnations are the symbol of the revolutionary coup that took place in 1974. There is a saying in Portuguese that "he who kisses my children sweetens my mouth," so if you are in doubt as to what to take and your hosts have small children, taking a gift for the children is a good alternative.

SPORTS CLUBS

With such a mild climate, Portugal is ideal for nautical or outdoor sports such as golf, tennis, or sailing. When someone practices one of these, it is common for the whole family to meet at the club on the weekend for lunch or to spend the day. Membership at the same club presupposes common interests and encourages familiarity. When in their clubs, people tend to be more at ease and ready to socialize with strangers. Gyms are also a good place to meet people and there are plenty around. Both clubs and gyms generally require a membership fee followed by monthly or annual payments.

EXPATRIATE CLUBS

Though the best way to blend in and get to know Portuguese culture is to mix with the locals, there are a number of expatriate clubs in the country's main cities that provide useful practical information and help one to settle in. In Porto, the port wine industry has created a sizeable British community. Aside from the British, there are also many German, Dutch, and South African immigrants who have settled along the beautiful Estoril coast, just west of Lisbon, and, of course, in the Algarve. The best way to obtain information about expatriate clubs is through the consulates and embassies.

ENGLISH-LANGUAGE PUBLICATIONS

There are two English-language newspapers published in Portugal: the *Portugal News* is weekly and has national coverage and distribution, also offering an online edition (www.theportugalnews. com). The *Portugal Resident* has a daily online publication (www.portugalresident.com) and three weekly regional editions focusing on the Algarve, greater Lisbon area and Madeira. Major international newspapers and magazines are widely available.

MANNERS: DOS AND DON'TS

There are a few principles that should be followed in order to avoid causing offense.

- Do not stretch or sprawl in public places, and never put your feet on top of furniture.
- Do not turn your back to someone you are in a group with; if this is unavoidable, excuse yourself beforehand.

- At the table, the knife is always in the right hand and pushes the food on to the fork, which remains in the left. These are used simultaneously. The North American habit of cutting the food first and then eating using only the fork in the right hand is considered bad manners.
- Once finished, place your knife and fork beside each other on the plate.
- Maintain good posture; keep both hands above the table and your napkin on your lap, using it regularly.
- It is acceptable to eat food such as shellfish with your fingers, but do not lick them!
- If you are unsure whether a dish applies as finger food, follow your host's example.
- Though smoking used to be very common in Portugal, anti-smoking legislation passed in 2014 making it illegal to smoke in all bars, restaurants, and nightclubs, as well as regular increases in tobacco tax, led many people to quit, and smoking is now much less widespread than it used to be. When in someone's home, it is best to ask permission before lighting up, or wait for someone else to light their cigarette first.

chapter five

THE PORTUGUESE AT HOME

PORTUGUESE HOMES

In the main cities and towns, most Portuguese live in apartments. These can vary from modest two-bedroom, one-bathroom homes in large apartment complexes to spacious five-bedroom flats in luxury

condominiums with communal garden and pool areas. Away from the urban centers, townhouses and villas (*vivendas*) with ground-level patios or gardens become more numerous. Due to rent laws that heavily favored the tenant over the landlord and made evicting difficult tenants a long and complicated process that most owners were not willing to risk, most homes used to be owned rather than rented. However, amendments made to the Urban Lease Law in 2012 enabling owners to update their rents and facilitate the eviction process, has resulted in a new and very dynamic rental market. Added to this, the lack of mortgage lending brought about by the economic crisis, has also forced many Portuguese to rent rather than buy their residences.

In addition, the government also implemented tax benefits to attract foreign investment and encourage property refurbishment (Golden Visas, Non-Habitual Residents Tax Regime and incentives to Urban Regeneration), and this has brought great vigor to the real estate market, with special impact on the rental sector. These measures, as well as a remarkable rise in tourism in Lisbon and Porto, created a wave of urban regeneration in the city centers and a new trend in short-term rental that has swept the property market. replace tile pic with old pic of appartments

Apartments and houses vary in degrees of comfort and charm according to age. The interest of foreign and national investment to renovate and renew Portugal's major cities has transformed once drafty and uncomfortable, but charming, old buildings into comfortable  dwellings fitted with modern comforts such as quality materials and central heating. The materials used depend on the region. In the north, more angular houses made primarily of stone and wood predominate, while in the south, rounded, whitewashed, Moorish-looking architecture is more common. Traditional blue and white Portuguese tile is used widely all over the country, especially in bathrooms and kitchens. Newly built homes are more comfortable and follow a streamlined, more minimalist vein, using modern materials and being equipped with central heating and better insulation.

Due to the urban centers being cramped and crowded, many people have a second home in the country or on the coast for weekends and vacations. These can range from a plot of land with a spacious home that provides escape from the small quarters of a city apartment, to an even smaller apartment on the coast, but with ocean views and a beach nearby. Those who do not have an alternative, but come to the city for work, may choose to spend weekends and vacations in their hometowns with extended families.

Beware of weekend traffic because people who have the option prefer to flee the city whenever they can, especially on public holidays or in the summer, when the downtown heat is stifling.

THE HOUSEHOLD

Housewife in Portuguese is *dona de casa*, which can be translated literally as "owner or lady of the house." Though the father is considered the head of the family, it is the mother who runs the home and carries the brunt of the domestic responsibility, even if she works. Women in Portugal are extremely house-proud and make a point of having a spotless and organized household. Though not competitive, when visiting other  homes, they will notice if these are clean and tidy and will comment if someone's house falls short of their standards, though not necessarily in the person's presence. Meals are usually cooked fresh every day and from scratch, since anything preprepared or frozen is frowned upon.

Aunties and In-Laws

After returning from their honeymoon and setting up house, newlywed couples are expected to entertain their respective families. Whether they have invited the whole family at once or a few at a time, young wives must rise to the occasion and be prepared for their female relatives and in-laws to leave no stone unturned. A complete tour of the new home must be given, and drawers, closets, and cabinets will most likely be inspected and scrutinized!

Diet varies from region to region, but most meals begin with soup, followed by a meat, fish, or poultry dish with rice or potatoes, and fruit for dessert. Fresh produce in Portugal is of excellent quality and requires little preparation, but the Portuguese also love heavier dishes stewed in olive oil or tomato-based sauces.

Breakfast and dinner are family affairs, with everyone eating together whenever possible. Breakfast is usually a light meal of bread, coffee, and milk, while dinner is heavier and considered the main family meal of the day. In the north, many families also come home from work and school for lunch; this is less common further south. Working mothers usually shop for groceries at the end of the day and prepare dinner when they get home, with the evening meal taking place at around 8:30 p.m. Toddlers generally eat earlier, and in this case parents may choose to have dinner after putting them to bed. Children and husbands seldom help around the house. This is changing, however, as women come to play a greater role in the workforce and have less time to dedicate to cooking and cleaning.

SHOPPING

The shopping center boom in the early 1990s brought with it the hypermarket trend. These large supermarkets are usually found in shopping

malls and have everything from food and
household products to clothes and sporting goods.
Low prices and long working hours (usually from
around 9:00 a.m. to 10:00 p.m.) make these stores
very popular for monthly or weekly shopping at
night or on the weekend.

For fresh produce and daily staples, people still
prefer their neighborhood shops. Bread is usually
bought from the bakery every morning. Fruit
and vegetables come from the local *mercearia*,
a small grocer, or from the municipal market
(*mercado*), which is open every day except
Monday from around 8:00 a.m. to 1:00 p.m.
Once a week most municipalities also have an
open-air market, the *feira*, that runs from early
morning to lunchtime, with gypsies and traders
selling clothes, accessories, kitchen utensils, baked
goods, and fresh food. Every neighborhood has at
least one pharmacy, and these take weekly turns

running a twenty-four-hour shift. The name and address of the establishment providing a night service is posted on all pharmacy windows. Small shops and pharmacies run from around 9:00 a.m. to 6:00 or 7:00 p.m. and close for two hours at lunchtime. Banking hours are usually from 8:30 a.m. to 3:00 p.m.; some branches, however, are open from 10:00 a.m. to 5:00 p.m. There is a large network of ATM machines (*multibanco*) that allow one not only to withdraw and deposit funds, but also to pay bills, transfer money, and even purchase train tickets.

DAILY LIFE

The day in Portuguese homes usually begins with family breakfast at around 8:00 a.m. After that, children are taken to school and parents go to work. During the workday there are plenty of coffee breaks. The first one takes place upon arrival at the office, with colleagues, among plenty of noise and activity at a nearby café. Another coffee is generally shared mid-morning, followed by a lunch break at around 1:00 p.m., which lasts approximately an hour and a half. There may be another coffee break mid-afternoon, with the day ending between 5:30 and 7:00 p.m. That said, it is important to note that punctuality is not a Portuguese virtue and it is common for people to be flexible with their working hours, starting and ending later than expected.

Once the workday has ended, most people head home. In the summer months, when daylight lasts until around 9:00 p.m., groups often get together for a drink on an esplanade at the end of the day, or children may be taken to the park or the beach.

Many urban centers lie on the coast and the waterfront areas have been well prepared for leisure and activities, so it is customary to see families out on bicycles or on foot, before or after dinner, enjoying the early evening.

The Portuguese love to socialize and go out, so restaurants and bars pick up the pace as early as Wednesday or Thursday, staying open until well after midnight and generally closing on Monday.

Coffee Culture

Portuguese life is fueled by coffee. Any excuse is a good one to take a coffee break, whether at home, at the office, or at a café, and people may drink coffee five or six times a day, though this is not recommended for those unaccustomed to a strong brew! Cafés are never empty, and the din around breakfast and lunchtime can make normal conversation impossible. Aside from the café culture, the coffee culture is also very strong, and the coffee in Portugal is of great quality. The main Portuguese brands are Nicola, Torrié, Sical, and Delta, the latter two holding by far the largest market share. These firms import the beans from Africa and South America and then produce

the coffee domestically. Foreign brands such as Buondi, Segafredo, and Lavazza are also widely available, and most homes also have a capsule coffee machine, such as Nespresso and other supermarket brands.

If you order a *café* you will receive a regular espresso in a small porcelain cup, but there are a number of terms the locals use to state their preference.

For instance, in Lisbon, a *bica* (pronounced "beeka") is also a term used to request a regular coffee, while in the north the locals may ask for a *cimbalino*, a word that derives from Cimbali, an Italian brand of espresso machines used in many establishments.

A *café curto* (literally meaning "short coffee") means the person wants their cup less full than the regular coffee, while an *italiana* is even shorter and very concentrated, with virtually only a shot of coffee.

A *café comprido* (literally "long coffee") is almost full to the brim, and can also be called *café cheio*, which means "full coffee."

Then there is the *carioca*, which is a weaker coffee since the grain has been slightly watered down. For this, a normal coffee has to be taken first and then the *carioca* is made, using the same blend from the previous coffee. Then there is what northerners call a *pingo*, literally meaning "a drop," which is a regular coffee with a drop of milk in it. In Lisbon, this is called a *garoto* (the literal translation of which is "little boy").

The Portuguese version of *café au lait* is called a *galão*, which is served in a tall glass, or a *meia de leite*, which literally translated means "half of milk," which is served in a mug. However, foreigners need not balk at this complex "Javanese"! If you simply order a *café,* you will be given a regular espresso, and if it's a traditional *café au lait* you'd like, ask for a *café com leite* (pronounced "late"). The above-mentioned varieties are also all available in decaffeinated versions—in Portuguese, *descafeinado*.

TELEVISION

Television is extremely popular in Portugal, and the TV set is often on for as long as there are people at home. The most popular programs are the news broadcasts, the beloved national and Brazilian soap operas, and reality shows. The soap operas (*novelas*) compete for television ratings with live soccer broadcasts and reality or talent shows such as "X-Factor," which are followed religiously and are hot topics of conversation in the cafés in the morning.

CHILDREN

Children are the center of the family, and from an early age accompany their parents everywhere, from restaurants and hotels to shopping malls and sometimes the office. Yet, like everything else in Portuguese society, their upbringing is at times boisterous and contradictory. Adults may be seen scolding children loudly and spanking them in public one moment, then hugging them vigorously and smothering them with kisses the next. Children must abide by strict rules of behavior and decorum, but then are indulged with material things and become avid consumers.

The children's upbringing is primarily left to the mother, who may rely greatly on help from the grandparents. Grandparents are often viewed as surrogate parents and have full authority over their grandchildren, but mothers are fiercely protective of their offspring and will not tolerate any form of aggression toward their child from other children or adults. Though public day care is available from the age of four months, mothers prefer, if possible, to leave their children at home with a family member or caretaker until the age of around three.

As in the rest of the world, with a growing educated middle class, changes are being felt in the home and parents have a more open and realistic attitude toward their adolescent children, although girls are still urged to guard their "reputation." In many households, parents are still uncomfortable discussing sex, although sexual education is taught in school as of grade 8 and families are adopting a more open attitude toward sexuality and sexual discussion. In the past, girls and boys were only expected to leave home when they married, but with more adolescents leaving home to attend university, young professionals concentrating more on their careers than in starting a family, and a greater acceptance of couples living together outside wedlock, the marrying age in Portugal has been rising steadily.

EDUCATION

The education system in Portugal used to be of poor quality in comparison with the rest of Europe, and it was common for Portuguese students to fail regularly and drag out their secondary and higher education over a number of years. This has improved over the last few decades, however, and the progress is visible.

School attendance is mandatory between the ages of six and eighteen, though many children start attending preschool at age three or earlier. Secondary education (from the age of fifteen) is mandatory. Public school fees are means-tested and set according to the family's income. For those who can afford them, there are also a large number of private and international schools.

The school year lasts from September to June, and a normal school day is a long one. Classes start between 8:30 and 9:00 a.m. and often run until 4:00 or 5:00 p.m. After classes, many children go on to various extracurricular activities.

There are numerous public and private universities in Portugal as well as many polytechnic institutes. Students who apply for higher education must complete a national (for public institutions) or local (for private institutions) entrance exam to qualify. Less than 20 percent of the student population continues on to higher education, but the Portuguese government has committed to create incentives to increase this number significantly in its Portugal 2020 program.

BUREAUCRACY

Obtaining even the most basic official documents in Portugal used to be an extremely lengthy and bureaucratic process. Lines were interminable, numerous photocopies and photographs were necessary, and a long wait before receiving the final document was guaranteed. People love to complain about the complication and tedium involved in the bureaucratic process, but do nothing about it and sometimes use a two-hour wait as an excuse to avoid going back to work. Though long waits can still be expected at the different government offices, for certain simpler matters, such as renewing a passport or driver's license, the government has opened a "one-stop shop" in most of the bigger cities. These "*Lojas do Cidadão*," which literally means "citizens' shop," usually speed up the process greatly. It is also now possible to take care of many bureaucratic services online, with relatively easy and efficient websites to manage everything from taxes to social security. Still, these are mostly only available in Portuguese, so be prepared to fill out many forms and to return more than once before all the necessary information is imparted.

MILITARY SERVICE

Military service was compulsory in Portugal until 2004, but after that year the armed forces were made fully professional. Nowadays young men are no longer obliged to participate in military training, but conscription for both men and women is implemented if insufficient people volunteer. Male citizens do receive a call notice

from the Ministry of Defense on the year they
turn eighteen to attend National Defense Day, a
full-day information session on national defense.

chapter six

TIME OUT

The Portuguese live for their family gatherings and social occasions, and this is especially evident during their free time. Any excuse is a good one to get together with family and friends, or to go to a club and participate in or watch sports activities. Food is taken very seriously, and socializing on any scale generally involves eating and drinking. People are often willing to make day or weekend trips just to savor a local delicacy. Meals are social occasions where sharing experiences and conversation is as important as enjoying the food.

In social situations, the Portuguese like to dress for the occasion, and shopping is a regular pastime. Women like to look stylish and actively follow trends. They will groom themselves just to leave the house, and even gym outfits are planned with care.

FOOD

Food in Portugal is steeped in history and tradition. Irrigation and gardening techniques dating back to Moorish times created the olive groves and vineyards that provide the ingredients at the center of the Portuguese diet. Vasco da Gama's discovery of the maritime route to the Far East brought a wide variety of spices that are still staples in every Portuguese kitchen, such as coriander, pepper, and paprika. The exploration of Africa and South America supplied the peppers, potatoes, vegetables, fruit, and coffee essential to most dishes and meals.

Seafood

The cold waters of the Atlantic provide a wealth of seafood, and Portugal's fish and shellfish are considered among the world's tastiest. One of the least expensive and most preferred fresh fish is the sardine, which can be seen and smelled grilling on barbecues all summer long and is the main feature on the *Santos Populares* menu. Grilled sardines are eaten plain with just olive oil drizzled over them, or on top of a chunk of fresh bread, with boiled potatoes and marinated roasted peppers as side dishes.

Dried, salted codfish is a regular several times a week in every Portuguese home. There are supposedly as many ways to cook cod (*bacalhau*) as there are days in the year, and most families

have their own favorite cod recipe that has been passed down from previous generations.

Shellfish is also popular, with dishes such as stuffed crab, hot or cold mussels (*mexilhões*), and clams (*ameijoas*) stewed in a variety of ways, always with plenty of garlic and fresh coriander. There are also many freshwater fish, such as the lamprey (*lampreia)* from the Minho region, which is considered a delicacy and is available only in the spring. The warmer waters of the Azores and Madeira provide their own species of seafood, such as *lapas*—crustaceans that cling to rocks—as well as all the traditional fresh fish, tuna being a favorite.

Meat Dishes

The Portuguese are very fond of meat, fowl, and game, with recipes varying according to each

region's local traditions. Smoked ham (*presunto*) and spicy *chouriço* sausages are everywhere. From the north come further delicacies such as roast lamb and suckling pig, as well as smoked pork, various sausages, and tripe dishes. Pork is also very popular in the Alentejo, where wheat abounds, along with olive and cork trees that release nuts and truffles for the pigs to enjoy.

All over the country, each region has its own version of *favas* and *feijoada*, two rich, aromatic stewed dishes comprised of beans and a variety of fresh and smoked meats. There is also the *cozido à Portuguesa*, where beef and pork are stewed in the same pot as a series of vegetables and herbs, again with individual regions adding their local touches. The year-round mild climate in the Azores and Madeira provides prime conditions for cattle to graze and a wide array of tropical fruits and vegetables to grow. Beef is tender and of excellent quality, and the local yams and cornbread are a must at every meal.

Mock Pork Sausages

One of Portugal's delicacies, produced mainly in the Trás-os-Montes region, is *alheira*, a smoked sausage fried in oil or baked in the oven and served with leafy greens, homemade fries, and fried egg—not exactly a light meal! The story behind these sausages dates back to the Inquisition, when Jews would make them with poultry flesh and fat, bread, garlic, and spices, and hang them in the window so that when the Inquisitors passed, they would assume the *alheiras* were regular pork sausages belonging to a non-Jewish household. *Alheira* is still a popular dish; however the modern versions do contain pork.

Soups

Soup is usually a part of lunch and dinner in Portuguese homes. Hot or cold soups are very popular in the Alentejo, and are substantial enough to serve as a main course, often including bread, beans, poached eggs, or even fish and meat.

Stone soup (*sopa da pedra*), which is a specialty of the Ribatejo region, is a rich, thick soup made from an assortment of beans, pork, *chouriço* sausage, vegetables, and spices.

Stone Soup

The fable of stone soup was written by
Teofilo Braga (1843–1924), a popular Portuguese
writer and politician. The story tells of a monk
who was begging from door to door. Starving
and having received nothing from yet another
household, he looked to the ground and picked
up a stone, cleaned it off, and claimed he would
then make stone broth. When the family laughed
at him, he feigned surprise and informed them
that the dish in question was very tasty. Curious,
the family said they wanted to watch him make
it, so the monk asked them for a pot, into which
he placed the stone and then filled with water. He
then asked them to place the pot on their stove
in order for the water to boil. Once the water had
boiled, the monk asked for some lard, followed
by salt, *chouriço*, and bread, all of which they
gave him. When he had finished eating the soup,
the family asked the monk about the stone at the
bottom of the pot, to which he replied that he
would be taking it with him for next time.

Cheese

From sheep, goat, and cow's milk come an impressive
variety of Portuguese cheeses. The textures vary
from rich and creamy to drier, harder cheeses, and
flavors range from delicate and mild to extremely
strong. Some cheeses are served as appetizers while
others come after a meal with port or red wine. Like

the traditional dishes, cheeses also change from region to region, with the buttery *Queijo da Serra* produced in the north, *Serpa* cheese from the Alentejo, and the parmesan-like *Queijo da Ilha* from the Azores.

Desserts

The Portuguese also have an extremely sweet tooth. In the seventeenth and eighteenth centuries, convents made their pastries famous by competing with each other to see who could produce the most divine desserts. This resulted in extremely delicate and rich cakes, pies, and puddings with very allusive names, such as *barriga de freira* ("nun's belly"), *toucinho do ceu* ("heaven's lard") and *pudim de abade de priscos* ("abbot's pudding"). From the Algarve come delicate marzipan desserts shaped like fruit,

fish, or seashells. Sweet egg paste is used in many desserts such as *Aveiro's ovos moles* (soft eggs) as well as the burnt custard seen in the famous Belém *pastel de nata* (cream pastry), whose recipe is still a well-guarded secret today.

Chicken *Piri-piri*

A healthier and tastier alternative to fast food in Portugal is chicken *piri-piri*, or *frango no churrasco*, which translated literally is barbecued chicken. *Piri-piri* is a hot sauce, but this chicken, found mainly in the greater Lisbon area, is available in both hot and non-spicy versions. Whole chickens are cut down the middle and placed spread-eagle on a spit over a coal barbecue. A chicken is removed from the spit to order, and is then brushed with either hot butter or a spicy sauce, whichever the customer prefers. In some of these establishments, you can sit at a table and eat your chicken there, while others offer a take-out service only.

WINE

Portugal has been exporting its wine since the Middle Ages, and has come to occupy an important position in today's international wine markets. With such an extensive variety, commercial wine production is heavily regulated and classified according to geographic origins and specific characteristics, with every phase of production

under strict control. The wine regions, officially known as *regiões demarcadas* (demarcated regions), indicate the wine's geographic origin as well as the attributes particular to that area.

Portuguese wines can be placed into two broad categories: VQPRD, which means Quality Wine Produced in a Determined Region, and Table wines. Bottles bearing the VQPRD seal contain quality wines produced in a specific demarcated region. In each region, local commissions regulate the production and classify the VQPRD wines as DOC (Denomination of Controlled Origin) or Regional.

DOC wines are produced in limited quantities and must follow strict rules of production regarding the variety, selection, geographic origin of the grapes, alcohol content, and specific vinification processes. They must also conform to certain standards of clarity, aroma, and flavor.

Regional wines are local wines produced in a specified region, but which do not follow the same strict rules of production as DOC wines.

Table wines are considered of lesser quality, do not have a geographic demarcation, and are not permitted to mention grape variety or the year of harvest on the label.

Vinho verde ("green wine"), a light, slightly sparkling wine ideal with seafood or just to cool down on a hot day, is produced only in Portugal along the Minho coast. Also in the north lies the Douro Valley, the oldest demarcated region in the world (since 1756), where some of the country's best full-bodied red wines are produced, as well as the world-renowned port wine. The valley can be visited by car, boat, or train and offers beautiful views of the wine family estates and terraced vineyards. Head downstream to Gaia, directly across the river from Porto, for wine tasting in the port wine cellars.

Toward the center of the country, vineyards run from the mountainous regions of the Dão and Bairrada to the flatter Ribatejo and Oeste (meaning west) region on the coast. Closer to Lisbon, the lush hills of Sintra produce the red wines of Colares, and toward Mafra lies Bucelas, which boasts some of the best Portuguese whites. Further south, the Costa Azul (Blue Coast) provides not only wonderful red and white wine but also the syrupy, sweet muscatel as well. In the south, the parched soils of the Alentejo and Algarve produce the fruity, apparently lighter wines that actually have an

alcoholic content sometimes higher than
13 percent. Madeira wine, the dessert wine
that originates from that region, has always been
very popular worldwide, especially in England.
It is said that in the fifteenth century, when
George, Duke of Clarence, was sentenced to
death for plotting to overthrow his brother the
king, Edward IV, he chose death by drowning in
a butt of Malmsey—sweet Madeira wine.

These main regions offer eleven well-planned
wine routes for those who wish to explore
Portuguese wine culture and landscapes: the
green wine route, the port wine route, the
Cister vineyards route, the Dão wine route,
the Bairrada wine route, the Beira Interior
wine route, the west wine route, the Ribatejo
vineyards route, the Bucelas, Carcavelos, and

Colares wine routes, the Costa Azul wine route, and the Alentejo wine route. All offer visits of varying lengths with many interesting tourism and wine-related activities.

EATING OUT

The Portuguese enjoy nightlife, and this usually begins with dinner. Eating out takes place even later than when dining at home, with many establishments serving until as late as 11:00 p.m. or midnight. Restaurants vary greatly in sophistication and menus, so it is a good idea to ask the locals for their suggestions, since a greasy-looking tavern (*tasca*) or grill (*churrasqueira*) can sometimes offer the best food in town. Many restaurants have menus in English and other languages, so be sure to ask. A lower-priced set tourist meal (*ementa turística*) consisting of an appetizer, main course, dessert, and a drink is also generally available and makes choosing easier.

Once you are seated, most restaurants will place bread, butter, olives, cheese, or some other variety of appetizers on the table. This is included in the cover charge and serves mainly to ease the wait involved after ordering, since fresh food will only be cooked once orders are placed. Vegetarian restaurants are not very common, but can be found in the major cities. Still, a wide variety of fresh vegetables and fish, as well as plenty of Italian and Asian restaurants, usually provides a tasty, meat-free alternative.

NIGHTLIFE

Portugal offers a varied and active nightlife with plenty of bars and nightclubs, also referred to as "discotheques," to choose from. These don't fill until after dinnertime, and often only really pick up around 1:00 or 2:00 a.m., staying open until 5:00 a.m. or later. Many discos charge an entrance fee that usually includes one free drink; otherwise, minimum consumption (also usually one drink) is imposed. In most discos, the customer is given a card upon entering on which all drinks are noted; payment is then carried out at the exit, so it is very

important not to lose the card or the maximum possible fee will be charged. On the streets outside the discos you will find trailers selling food such as hamburgers and hotdogs, and the night can go on until early morning.

TIPPING

There is no set rule when it comes to tipping in restaurants in Portugal, and tips are not usually included in the bill. The Portuguese generally tip between 0 and 5 percent, but foreigners are expected to leave around 10 percent. It is not customary to tip in bars or cafés, and in taxis the price is usually just rounded up to the nearest euro.

SHOPPING FOR PLEASURE

On the weekend, the large shopping centers fill to the brim with entire families browsing, eating, and shopping the day away. These malls are open seven days a week from 10:00 a.m. to 11:00 p.m., or sometimes later, and offer a large selection of well-known national and international brands, food, and cinema.

For more traditional, open-air shopping, downtown areas (*baixa*) have pedestrian-only cobblestone streets lined with shops and cafés. Here anything from major brands to "typical" Portuguese arts and crafts can be found. These shops also open at 10:00 a.m., some closing for lunch between 1:00 p.m. and 3:00 p.m. and then reopening until 7:00 p.m. On Saturdays, many smaller or local shops close for the day at 1:00 p.m. Government-regulated sales take place

twice yearly, in January/February and August/
September. Good buys for visitors in Portugal
include clothes and shoes, tiles and ceramics,
and wine.

BANKS
Portugal's currency was the *escudo* until 1999,
when the country became one of the eleven
founding members of the euro. Apart from
exchange desks at airports, foreign currency must
be changed through a bank. There are many in
the city centers and they are easily recognizable.
Banking hours are from 8:30 a.m. to between
3:00 p.m. and 5:00 p.m, depending on the branch,
and there is a large network of ATM machines
available twenty-four hours a day. The main

The Barcelos Cockerel

The Barcelos cockerel has become a popular Portuguese mascot and is a recurrent motif in local handicrafts. The legend that made the rooster famous begins with a mysterious crime in Barcelos that left the townspeople shaken and afraid. When a pilgrim from Galicia passed through the town, allegedly on his way to Santiago de Compostela, the locals were quick to arrest him and condemn him for the crime. Before his execution, the Spaniard asked to be taken before the judge to plead his innocence. He was admitted to the judge's residence where a banquet was about to take place. Pointing to a roasted rooster on the table, the condemned man claimed that should he be innocent, the cooked cockerel would crow as he was being hanged. Sure enough, as he was about to hang, the rooster stood up on the table and crowed! The Spaniard was immediately set free, returning to Barcelos years later to raise a monument honoring the Virgin Mary and Saint James.

Portuguese banks are Caixa Geral de Depositos, Millennium-BCP, and Novo Banco.

SPORTS

Without a doubt, the most popular sport in Portugal is soccer. Each town has its own team and playing field, but the main rivals are Benfica (Lisbon), Sporting (Lisbon), and FC Porto. When a game takes place between any of these teams, the country comes to a standstill as everyone watches live or on television, and afterward the winning team's fans take to the streets to celebrate victory. Though people are fiercely loyal to their teams, outbursts of violence such as those seen in the United Kingdom are very rare. Fans may provoke each other, and the occasional skirmish may break out, but these situations usually subside without the need for police intervention.

Portuguese soccer teams and players are considered among the best in the world, with legends such as Eusebio, Figo, and Cristiano Ronaldo winning international recognition.

Hosting Euro 2004 put Portugal on the world's soccer map, and the country rose to the occasion by improving urban infrastructures and building several large, state-of-the-art stadiums. When in 2016 Portugal won the UEFA championship for the first time in the thrilling final played in the Stade de France in Paris, a wave of national pride took hold of the country.

Four-hundred and ninety-seven miles (800 km) of coastline and mild weather make Portugal an ideal place to practice water sports. The country's beaches, such as Guincho (near Estoril) and Ericeira (near Mafra), offer some of the best surfing and windsurfing conditions in Europe and host international championships every year.

Yacht clubs all over the country are also busy all year-round organizing sailing events for every class of boat, from the smaller Olympic classes such as Laser to large sailboats. In 2004 Portugal was one of the contenders to host the America's

Cup regatta on the Lisbon coast, making it to the final decision stages but losing in the end to the Spanish town of Valencia. In 2007 the prestigious ISAF Sailing World Championship took place in Cascais, and Lisbon was the first stop in the 2011–2012 America's Cup World Series Regattas.

Tennis courts can be found in most towns all over the country. Resorts in the Algarve, Madeira, and Estoril offer tennis holidays,

and every year the Portugal Open is included in the ATP World Tours calendar, attracting international players and fans.

Portuguese golf courses are considered among the finest in Europe, and in 2014, the World Golf Awards named Portugal the World's Best Golf Destination. The better-known courses are in the Algarve and Estoril area, but there is also a wide selection along the west coast and in the northern part of the country.

The Portuguese enjoy an early morning or evening walk, run, or bike ride, and many city dwellers can be seen taking to the seaside

promenades prepared for this kind of activity.
For longer strolls, visit one of the many
nature reserves, such as Sintra, Peneda-Gerês,
Montesinho, and Madeira, and enjoy the dense,
green landscapes on foot or bicycle.

VACATIONS

Many businesses close for all or part of the month
of August, and most Portuguese take this time
for their vacations as well. Vacations are generally
spent en masse with friends and family. Those
who have second homes or are away from their
hometowns take the opportunity to enjoy these
spots at a more leisurely pace. For those who
choose to get away and rent accommodation,
once an adequate destination is found, it will
usually be revisited every year.

Large Portuguese communities in France,
Germany, Switzerland, and Canada bring about
an influx of emigrants who return to their
hometowns for their summer and Christmas
vacations, as well as family members in Portugal
who travel to those countries to visit loved
ones living abroad. Another favorite holiday
destination is Brazil, a warm break from the
damp and chilly Portuguese winters.

With such an inviting coastline, however,
virtually everyone takes to the Portuguese
beaches for their summer vacations. In the
north, the ocean is rougher and cold, and

the climate is less predictable, with summer mornings that tend to be quite misty and chilly. In the south, warmer water, sunny skies, and high temperatures are guaranteed, making the Alentejo and Algarve beaches among the most popular. This popularity has rendered the Algarve extremely busy and crowded in the summer months. As an alternative, the discerning visitor could head north to discover the cooler temperatures and charm of the Minho and Douro regions.

CULTURAL ACTIVITIES

In 1994, Lisbon was the European Union's culture capital, followed by Porto in 2001, and Guimarães in 2012; Lisbon also hosted Expo '98. These events not only broadened the country's cultural horizons, but also raised awareness of Portuguese culture abroad. There are several well-respected foundations, such as the Gulbenkian in Lisbon and Serralves in Porto, which show the work of local artists and international touring companies. The Centro Cultural de Belém in Lisbon and the Casa da Música in Porto house impressive and modern auditoriums that offer a varied choice of national and foreign dance and music programs.

Popular culture is a favorite in Portugal. Most major pop and rock artists pass through Lisbon or Porto or both, filling stadiums to capacity. The cinema is also very popular, with many Hollywood films making it to the Portuguese screens, playing in the original version with Portuguese subtitles. Portuguese cinema is of excellent quality but still relatively unknown, and of course there is the language barrier. Still, artists like Joaquim de Almeida, Maria de Medeiros and Marisa Cruz have achieved international recognition, as did the film director Manoel de Oliveira, who was recognized with several international awards at prestigious events such as the Berlinale, Golden Globes and Cannes Film Festival, and worked with celebrities like John Malkovich and Catherine Deneuve.

The Glass Route

The Glass Route, in the Estremadura e Ribatejo region, aims to promote the area's rich glass manufacturing tradition. Five glass manufacturers and two museums have joined the Fatima/Leiria tourism board in this project to offer a tour of the area and display the history of Portuguese glasswork, which dates back to the beginning of the eighteenth century, as well as the craft and techniques used in the making of glass and crystal. In 1769, an Englishman named William Stephens took over the management of the failing Marinha Grande Royal Glass factory, going on to make it one of the most prestigious factories in the land.

chapter seven

TRAVEL, HEALTH, & SAFETY

ENTERING THE COUNTRY

Citizens of countries in the European Union, traveling to Portugal require only a valid identity card. Visas are not required for citizens of countries included in the Schengen area or those who have signed conventions with Portugal (ex. Brazil, Canada, Colombia).

Travelers from non EU countries over the age of seventeen may bring in the following duty-free items: two bottles of table wine, one bottle of hard liquor, 200 cigarettes or 250 grams of tobacco or fifty cigars, and 1.75 ounces of perfume. It is forbidden to enter the country carrying fresh meat. Drug use (other than medical drugs) is illegal. The legal age for both driving and alcohol consumption is eighteen.

FLYING

Portugal's national airlines operating domestic, European, and intercontinental routes are TAP and Sata, while TAP Express (former Portugalia)

operates nationally and within Europe. Most of the major international airlines fly to and from Portugal as well. On the continent, the main airports for domestic and international commercial flights are located in Faro, Lisbon, and Porto. In Madeira, there are airports in Funchal and Porto Santo, and the Azores airports are on Santa Maria, São Miguel (Ponta Delgada), and Terceira (Lajes). Besides these, there are numerous small airports that handle short-haul domestic flights, but the Lisbon and Porto airports account for more than 70 percent of the country's overall air traffic.

TRAINS

Portugal's national railway company, CP (Caminhos de Ferro Portugueses), offers extensive daily regular and express options for traveling up and down the country. The high-speed Alfa Pendular route between Braga and Faro is considered one of the best

intercity connections in Europe, and is the fastest way to reach the major northern or southern cities from Lisbon. For a more leisurely trip, there are regional trains that stop at most stations en route, and intercity trains that stop only at the main cities. Trains heading north leave from Lisbon's Santa Apolónia and Oriente stations. In Porto, passengers can disembark at Campanhã or São Bento, or continue on to stations further north. Southbound trains from Lisbon leave from the Barreiro station on the south side of the Tagus and end in the Algarve. There are also broad networks of local commuter trains.

Train travel in Portugal is cheap in comparison with other European countries. The Alfa, Regional, and Intercity trains offer first- and second-class cars. On all trains, children under the age of three travel free, and those between the ages of four and eleven travel for half the adult fare. Seven-, fourteen-, or twenty-one-day tickets are available at reduced rates for unlimited travel throughout the country.

International trains run daily from Lisbon and Porto to Paris (Sud Express), Madrid (Lusitânia), and Vigo. Portugal is also on the InterRail circuit, which links over thirty European countries.

BUSES

Coach travel is also a viable option, with a number of private operators running regular, comfortable, and affordable services.

Rede-Expressos links Lisbon to the main cities of Porto and Braga in the north, and Faro in the south. Renex, a Braga-based company, runs a regular Porto–Lisbon–Algarve route, with departures from the Clérigos Tower, one of Porto's most famous monuments. REDM specializes in the north, running a regular Porto to Bragança route, connecting with Coimbra and Lisbon as well. EVA runs regular routes between Lisbon, Alentejo, and the Algarve.

Bridges and Barges

The commuter traffic to and from Lisbon, the country's principal business center, can be staggering, especially for those who need to cross the Tagus. The 25 de Abril bridge (called the Salazar bridge until 1974), which looks very much like San Francisco's Golden Gate suspension

bridge, was inaugurated in 1966 and provided a quick and easy way to cross the river until the ever growing number of cars eventually turned it into a bottleneck for heavy traffic. In 1999, a lower railway level was added as a way to relieve congestion and provide an alternative to car travel. Another great feat of Portuguese civil engineering is the Vasco da Gama bridge. Inaugurated for the World Expo in 1998, at over 10 miles (17.2 km), it is the longest suspension bridge in Europe. Other than these two bridges, several docks along the Lisbon waterfront service a fleet of fast and modern ferries that provide regular river crossings.

DRIVING

Up until the early 1990s, the roads in Portugal were bad enough to make even the most adventurous tourist reconsider driving beyond a 20-mile (32-km) radius. Since then, however, thanks to events like the Lisbon and Porto European Culture Capital tenures, Expo '98, and Euro 2004, the network of new roads and highways is excellent and well-signed, making car travel virtually anywhere quick and easy. That said, it is a good idea to carry a GPS or detailed, up-to-date map and plan your route carefully before leaving, since once off highways and main roads, signage can be confusing or even nonexistent.

The Portuguese are reputedly among the most reckless drivers in Europe, and the accident rate is astounding. Generally rowdy and aggressive behind the wheel, this is the one time that Portuguese people are always in a hurry, so they tend to overuse their horns as well as their hands and voices. The best advice is to stay calm, maintain a sense of humor, and stick to the right lane. Give others the right of way, even if they're not entitled to it, because they will seldom yield. Most cars in Portugal are still standard transmission, so if you want to rent an automatic vehicle, be sure to specify this when booking with the rental agency.

The car is a prized possession in Portugal. Most people dream of owning one, if only to drive the family around on the weekend. This can make getting around by car on Saturday and Sunday afternoons very frustrating, especially along coastal roads and in small towns, since these fill with cars that circulate at virtually a walking pace, taking their time to enjoy the views and the drive.

Pedestrians beware! Though pedestrians have the right of way at crosswalks, drivers frequently ignore this, so be especially careful when crossing busy streets. If driving, watch out for jaywalkers—they come in large numbers and tend to cross anywhere, regardless of traffic.

Parking

The Portuguese have not taken to the concept of carpooling, so most cars carry only the driver. This causes traffic jams and bottlenecks on highways as well as in the urban centers, and makes above-ground parking very difficult to find. There are, however, many new underground parking lots spread throughout the cities.

The Portuguese are very creative and liberal with their parking, often occupying pedestrian crossings and pavements haphazardly, as well as gently nudging other bumpers in order to fit into a tight spot. As with driving, though, parking violations are also receiving greater attention and penalties. Parking is illegal on curbs marked with a yellow line. In some cases, an illegally parked car will receive only a ticket, but it is becoming more common for tow trucks to impound vehicles, and a wheel-clamping system has been introduced in the major city centers. If you are lucky enough

Parkers

Over the last few years a new phenomenon has arisen in the Portuguese urban centers. Homeless people have taken to the main streets and populated areas to "help" drivers find parking for their cars. These parking assistants are often seen waving at empty spaces, with the expectation of receiving monetary compensation for their efforts (usually a 50 cent or 1 euro coin). Giving them money is optional, but if you choose not to, there is always a chance you will find your car scratched or missing a mirror or antenna when you return. Even if you do give money, illegal parking spaces remain illegal and subject to fines, towing, or tire clamping, and parking meters must still be paid.

to find legal street parking, don't be surprised if passersby stop to watch you maneuver, and even join in to help out with signals and indications.

RULES OF THE ROAD

The Portuguese police used to have a notoriously laid-back attitude toward traffic regulations. This is no longer true. Today's laws have, in fact, become quite strict, and are aggressively enforced.

All passengers must, by law, wear seat belts. Children under the age of twelve must use appropriate car seats.

It is illegal to use cell phones while driving, except with an earpiece or hands-free set. It is also illegal to drive barefoot or without a shirt.

In case of a breakdown, the mandatory triangle must be placed on the road behind the car, and a green fluorescent jacket must be worn. These are provided in a rental car.

DRUNK DRIVING

The maximum legal limit for drinking and driving is 0.5 grams of alcohol per liter of blood. If this limit is exceeded, the penalties range from serious fines, immediate impoundment of the vehicle, and license suspension, to prison sentences.

When stopped by the police, the driver must submit a passport or other valid picture identification, a valid Portuguese or international driver's license (with photograph), vehicle registration, proof of ownership, and valid insurance papers. Most traffic police officers have weak foreign language skills, so if you do get stopped, chattering away in a foreign language might well get you off the hook, as long as it is for a minor offense.

Traffic regulations and road signs are the same in Portugal as in the rest of Europe. Driving is on the right-hand side. One should therefore circulate in the right lane and use the left lane only to pass or turn left. The Portuguese seldom obey this rule, but it is a good one to follow in order to avoid trouble. At junctions, vehicles approaching from the right always have priority, unless they encounter a stop or yield sign. At traffic circles, cars already on the circle have priority. Let them pass before you enter.

SPEED LIMITS

Built-up city area 31 miles per hour (50 kmph)

Main roads 56 miles per hour (90 kmph)

Highways 75 miles per hour (120 kmph)

Tolls

All highways have tolls, and the amount paid depends on the distance traveled. The shorter highways have a fixed rate, which is paid immediately, while longer distances will require you to collect a ticket at the first tollbooth and pay when exiting. Stop at the booth marked with a green light. All tollbooths have at least one fast lane identified with a white "V" inside a green

square. These are only for cars with an electronic toll payment system. Do not use these lanes unless your vehicle has the white toll identification box on the windshield.

URBAN TRANSPORTATION

Lisbon has an efficient underground rail system with four lines: red, blue, green, and yellow. The metro (marked with a white "M" in a red square) is clean, efficient, and inexpensive, and covers most of the city's center and outskirts, also connecting with buses and commuter trains. All stations have automatic ticket machines with easy-to-follow multilingual instructions. Lisbon's metro was extended and refurbished for Expo '98, and the new station terminals boast impressive tile murals by renowned Portuguese artists. In Porto, the under and above-ground metro has six lines that connect the city center with the surrounding

suburbs. Both Lisbon and Porto metros run between 6:00 a.m. and 1:00 a.m.

In Lisbon, Carris runs an extensive network of buses, streetcars, and cable cars. Bus stops are identified by posts or shelters displaying maps with the routes and timetables. There are several options for tickets and passes, the most popular among tourists being the Lisboacard, which includes one-, two-, or three-day travel passes plus free admission to certain monuments and museums.

In Porto, STCP runs the buses, streetcars, and cable cars. As in Lisbon, stops have posts or shelters that display route maps and timetables, and the Andante card allows use not only of the STCP transportation, but also of the metro and trains running in and around the city.

Until Portugal's entry into the European Union, taxis used to be black with green tops; while there are still some of these around, most taxis are now

all beige, as in much of Europe. The base fare
is always the same, but there are four different
tariffs, depending on the time of day or day of
the week (nights, weekends, and holidays being
most expensive). Extra is charged for phoned-
in requests and for luggage exceeding certain
dimensions, but portable child beds, strollers,
and wheelchairs are transported free of charge.
Within the cities and towns, the taxi's meter
must be running, but for longer distances the
fare is negotiated in advance and the passenger
is required to pay the taxi's return trip as well as
all tolls.

WHERE TO STAY

While Portugal offers a wide range of national and
international hotels on the mainland and islands,
with prices and services ranging from basic to
luxurious, there are a number of more "typical"
accommodation solutions that provide a better
taste of Portuguese culture. These are spread
evenly throughout the country.

Pousadas are state-owned historical buildings
such as castles, monasteries, and convents that
have been restored and turned into exclusive
hotels. These offer high service standards while
maintaining a strong cultural and regional
context.

Estalagens are four- or five-star hotels whose
architecture and style also reflect the regional

character. Unlike the *pousadas*, however, they are privately owned.

For more affordable accommodation, there are pensions (two to four stars), motels (two or three stars), and numerous youth hostels. Another popular choice for families is the *aparthotel*, a hotel consisting of self-contained apartment suites ranging from two to five stars, with living rooms and kitchenettes. Here visitors can settle in a more homelike environment. In 2012, Portugal introduced important reforms to an extremely outdated lease law which, in addition to attractive tax benefits for foreigners, brought a veritable boom to a virtually non-existent rental market. One of the effects of this was the mushrooming of short-term rental apartments, a phenomenon that has swept most major European cities, providing an alternative option for affordable tourist accommodation. With tourism booming even more than the real estate market, a wave of new hotel developments has also taken place in Portugal, bringing innovative new alternatives for families and young travelers.

For a more rural and family-oriented setting, there are TER (*turismo no espaço rural*) guesthouses. These are generally family-owned manor houses or working farms that provide contact with nature and the locals. They must be registered at the State Tourist Office and receive one of three classifications. TH (*turismo de habitação*) accommodation refers to manor houses recognized for their architectural value, TR (*turismo rural*) guesthouses are homes that reflect the rural environment, and AT (*agroturismo*) means that the accommodation is part of a farming estate. Every TER guesthouse must have a metal plaque in the main entrance displaying the TER symbol and State Tourist Office logo.

SOME MAJOR SITES	
Lisbon	**Porto**
Jeronimos Monastery	Clerigos Tower
Belem Tower	Serralves Foundation
Saint George Castle	Casa da Música
Alfama	Douro riverside

HEALTH

The Portuguese state provides national residents with free health care in public hospitals and health centers, but these are usually overcrowded, and the quality is sometimes questionable. Private health care in Portugal is undoubtedly a superior, albeit expensive option for foreigners, so it is best to acquire medical insurance before traveling.

Though many doctors speak English and/or French, it is best to have someone bilingual accompany you to help with communication, especially in an emergency situation. The national emergency phone number is 112, but, again, it is best to ask a local to place the call. It is also a good idea for foreigners to register with their embassy or consulate upon arrival and keep the number close at hand, just in case.

SAFETY

The Polícia de Segurança Pública (PSP) upholds security in the urban centers, while the Guarda Nacional Republicana (GNR) maintains national safety and runs the highway patrol (Brigada de Trânsito).

Violent crime is not a major threat in Portugal, though theft is common. To avoid problems, lock all doors and windows (cars, hotel rooms, home) and never leave bags or luggage unattended. Keep purses and wallets close to your body, and in hotel rooms and cars, do not leave money and valuable goods in plain sight. As with anywhere else in Europe, the usual commonsense precautions apply.

BUSINESS
BRIEFING

THE BUSINESS CULTURE

Portugal is a country of contrasts and
contradictions, and this is especially true in the
professional arena. The business fabric is very
diverse, even within the same field, with small,
family-run businesses at one end of the spectrum
and large multinationals at the other. Tempting
as it may be to try to generalize and stereotype
the business sphere, it is important to adapt your
approach and attitude to the particular company
with which you are dealing.

The average Portuguese employee upholds a "work to live" rather than a "live to work" ethic. The office is where one goes to make a living, while the more important aspects of life take place elsewhere. In business, as in their private lives, the Portuguese are individualistic and tend to concentrate on short-term rewards rather than long-term results. They are generally reluctant to take risks for fear of negative consequences, and avoid taking responsibility, passing decisions along to those in superior positions.

This apparent lack of accountability or commitment can be exasperating, but if successfully motivated and won over, Portuguese people are hardworking and fiercely loyal. In order to obtain cooperation, it is important to give the business at hand a personal angle; you should ask the person for their help rather than make them feel that they are fulfilling an obligation. When this is achieved, their resourcefulness and flexibility will surface, but only if they feel that they are helping themselves or doing someone a personal favor, rather than handling a professional situation.

Desenrascado

Portugal's business fabric is comprised primarily of small and medium-sized companies, or PMEs (*pequenas e médias empresas*), as the Portuguese call them. Many of these have been family-run for generations, with leadership passed on to relatives with little or no formal business training. For this reason, the Portuguese work ethic and habits can strike outsiders as unconventional and quite unprofessional. On the other hand, this unpredictable infrastructure, where job descriptions are often unclear, has made the Portuguese very good at multitasking, and extremely resourceful at problem solving. This flexibility and ability to think and act quickly under pressure, referred to in Portuguese as being "*desenrascado*," is a highly regarded characteristic. The more d*esenrascado* you are, the more respect you will command.

Cunhas

Another vital feature in business is connections, or "*cunhas*" (pronounced "*coonias*"). A suspicious people by nature, the Portuguese rely heavily on networking and connections to open doors. In many companies, to their own detriment, who you know is still more important than what you know, and the higher up in the organization your acquaintance is, the better. Name-dropping is common practice, and people show how well connected they are, or find out how well connected others are, by doing just that.

The main industries that have resulted from tradition and favorable natural conditions are textiles, footwear, cork, pulp and paper, wine, and tourism. Recently, however, other business areas have evolved, such as the auto and electronics industries, thus paving the way for new business trends. The growing influx of multinational organizations has also substantially broadened horizons and raised business standards and practices, as well as bringing a boom in the business services sector.

LABOR

In many ways, the Portuguese population's character traits carry over into the country's workforce: unambitious and undemanding, yet loyal and resourceful. Overall, unionization levels are low, even in the traditional heavy industry sectors such as metalwork, chemicals, and shipyards, and contact between the workers and syndicates is minimal. Curiously, the unionization level is unusually high in the banking sector (over 80 percent), due mostly to the special access provided to private medical care. The unions intervene very little in daily management and rarely exercise their right to information in various administrative decisions. Their role is more to oversee collective agreements and ensure these are implemented accordingly.

There are two national syndicates, the CGTP and the UGT, and these differ greatly politically and socially. The CGTP, the more activist union, represents primarily the blue-collar industry and public service sectors. The UGT focuses more on the private business sphere, with wider

representation of white-collar workers, such as
in the service and tourism sectors. Alternatively,
individual companies may choose to develop
their own labor policies and programs, using
government laws as a starting point.

COMPANY STRUCTURE AND ORGANIZATION

Most Portuguese firms are either corporations,
Sociedade Anónima (S.A.), or private limited
companies, Limitada (Lda.). Organizations
generally have a pyramid infrastructure, with an
administrator or board of directors at the top,
followed by the general manager, middle managers,
and employees at the bottom. This hierarchy is
rigid, clearly defined, and strictly followed. People
do not step on each other's toes, so one must
go through all the appropriate channels and be
prepared to wait to get even the simplest tasks
accomplished.

A typical workday begins anywhere between
8:30 a.m. and 10:00 a.m., depending on the type
of business, and ends between 4:30 p.m. and
7:00 p.m. The Portuguese are not known for their
punctuality, however, so although foreigners are
expected to be on time, they in turn should be
prepared to wait! Plenty of coffee breaks are taken
throughout the day, and lunches can last over
two hours. When in Portugal for business, stay
alert, since negotiations and other matters may

suddenly be resumed during these supposed timeouts. Deciding when to end the day can prove tricky. While leaving early or on time is met with disapproval, those who remain the latest are seldom the most productive.

Deadlines are considered a necessary formality not to be taken too seriously or literally, and are rarely met. Be sure to set a date that allows some leeway to get the job done when you need it. Even once a delivery date is established, phone ahead to ensure your business has not been forgotten or placed on the back burner.

CONTRACTS AND FULFILLMENT

Care should be taken when drafting and agreeing upon contracts. Portugal's legal system is based on Roman civil law and the Napoleonic Code, in which a complete existing body of law is applied to all cases. Portuguese contracts are therefore shorter and simpler than those drawn up under British common law because certain areas are already covered by the country's civil code. That said, growing foreign business and investment has brought a more Anglo-Saxon influence to some contracts in Portugal, thereby making them more extensive. US and British contracts, based on common law, tend to be longer and more elaborate because of the need to cover every eventuality.

Though this varies from sector to sector and company to company, contracts in Portugal are generally regarded as binding. However, in a country where a gentleman's agreement and a handshake still carry weight, it is not always necessary to revise contracts to cover small details. The Portuguese are not litigious by nature and will give each other the benefit of the doubt if the need for a small alteration arises. As we have seen, however, deadlines are often missed, even when stipulated in a contract, so be sure to set clauses that protect you in case of delays (for example, penalties or termination of the contract).

COMMUNICATION STYLE
Portuguese written communication in business tends to be formal and long-winded, though this has changed with the briefer e-mail medium.

During first meetings, the Portuguese adopt a certain formality and stiffness as much as a sign of respect as to indicate where each stands on the hierarchical ladder. With such a delineated hierarchy, the boss (*patrão*) tends to condescend to employees, and in return is accustomed to a degree of flattery and praise. If managed with subtlety, this is expected and appreciated.

Titles carry great significance in Portugal, and it is important to use them. Anyone with a generic university degree is entitled to use "Doctor," so at work Maria Silva will be referred to as "Maria Silva." If someone has a more technical degree, then that title is used. A male architect is called "*Senohor Arquitecto,*" a female engineer "*Senohora Engenheira,*" a male professor " *Senohor Professor.*" and so on. Although the entry of a great number of multinational companies in Portugal, as well as the emergence of new companies run by a younger generation, have reduced the formality in business environments, it is safer to maintain the more respectful *você* form in professional situations, unless your partner switches to the *tu* form (see Chapter 9). Do not call someone by their first name unless they insist or do the same.

Keep it Personal

Begin face-to-face or telephone communication by showing interest in the person's general well-being and personal life. The more details you remember (birthdays, children's ages), the more the person will warm to you. The Portuguese have a penchant for talking about their ailments in vivid detail, so inquiring about their health is guaranteed to score points. Also offer personal information about yourself, telling something about your life, family, or country. Take the time to engage in conversation and find common ground with the people with whom you intend to work, thereby creating a personal as well as professional relationship.

PRESENTATIONS AND NEGOTIATIONS

The Portuguese welcome presentations as a break from the regular work routine, but before long will begin worrying about how this is going to extend their workday. Thus, it is important to keep presentations short and to the point. Be confident and self-assured, without being cocky. Make eye contact and be prepared to negotiate down from your opening bid. Visual aids can be useful and create a good impression, but avoid distractions or anything that may prolong the presentation.

As a general rule, the decision-making process in Portuguese companies is highly centralized, and ultimately the responsibility of the managerial or administrative levels. With such a clear hierarchical structure, it is usually easy to determine who the decision maker is in a group. Concentrate the arguments on that person, though not in a way that disregards the other people present. Once you are past the presentation phase, be prepared to wait. The fear of taking responsibility for making the wrong decision is great, and all other options and alternatives will be explored before a final decision is made.

TEAMWORK

Given their strong hierarchical structure and inherently individualistic nature, teamwork is not a prominent feature in traditional Portuguese companies. That said, with the business fabric undergoing great expansion due to foreign investment and a budding service sector, the workforce is also evolving and adopting more inclusive and participative work methods. The dynamic young professionals who embody the new,

modern Portuguese companies fully embrace teamwork. In the older companies, where change is taking place more slowly, the importance of family and social life makes being part of a team come naturally, but be sure to define each team member's responsibilities clearly.

DRESS CODE

The dress code in business depends greatly on the field in question. Whereas in finance or law a formal business style of dress is adopted, in areas like advertising or telecommunications, people are more laid-back. When in doubt, it is safest to err on the side of business formality, with men wearing a suit or blazer and tie, and women avoiding short skirts and low-cut tops. Also refrain from wearing jeans and sneakers.

BUSINESS ENTERTAINING

The Portuguese love to socialize and entertain, so make yourself available for meals and drinks. While it is not uncommon to be invited to someone's home to meet the family, most business entertaining takes place in the country's best restaurants. Bear in mind that many deals are closed across the dinner table. A relaxed atmosphere takes the edge off business, and the Portuguese are very good at using this to their advantage. As for the bill, whoever entertains, pays. Thus, a foreigner visiting Portugal is considered a guest, but if a second visit is made, you should reciprocate.

WOMEN IN BUSINESS

Women have made great progress in the business world, especially where equal opportunity is concerned, with a growing number of women assuming top positions in companies and politics. The general consensus, however, is that attitudes have not really changed and men still have the upper hand in the professional arena, with a gender wage gap of around 9 percent. Thus women must make a much stronger effort to be heard in the boardroom, and their professional progression is much slower than that of their male counterparts, although this situation has evolved in newer or higher profile professions, such as the services sector, or in law, and finance. Nonetheless, once a woman has children, it is generally agreed that her career will slow down significantly, and Portugal is especially backward in this respect. Paid maternity leave is a mere five months, and there are very few incentives to keep a working mother in the workplace. Part-time or freelance jobs are frowned upon, as is working from home, yet day-care facilities on company premises are virtually nonexistent.

COMMUNICATING

THE PORTUGUESE LANGUAGE

Portuguese, spoken by an estimated 260 million people, is the official language in seven countries around the globe. These are Portugal, Brazil, Angola, Mozambique, Guinea-Bissau, Sao Tomé and Príncipe, and Cabo Verde. The language is also still widely spoken in former colonies such as Macao, East Timor, and Goa.

The Portuguese language has its earliest roots in Latin and Galician, with influences from Germanic and Arab dialects. During the Renaissance, its vocabulary and grammatical structure was further enriched by Greek. In the fifteenth century, extensive maritime travel brought contact with French and English, which would also contribute to modern Portuguese.

European Portuguese is a difficult language to learn. It is fast and throaty, and is curiously often confused with Slavic languages such as Russian or Polish. The Portuguese speak quickly, with vowels or even entire syllables "eaten up" or lopped off for the sake of brevity. A colorful range of slang and popular expressions makes the language even more challenging to understand. Still, though accents vary from north to south, the situation is not like that found in Spain, where the number of dialects renders the language incomprehensible from region to region. The main regional differences in Portuguese lie in pronunciation and popular expressions. In the north, the letter "v" is pronounced "b," and vice versa. In Madeira and the Azores, the accent is completely different, but with such a regular flow of tourists visiting all year-round, many of the locals speak rudimentary English.

Most language schools abroad offer Brazilian Portuguese rather than European Portuguese, probably because the former is easier to speak and understand. It is hard to believe that Brazilian is actually the same language. It is spoken much more slowly, with every letter and syllable enunciated and sung, rather than barked out like European Portuguese. The difference between the two could be compared to European French and Quebecois. Passionate about Brazilian TV soap operas, virtually all Portuguese understand Brazilian and are good at imitating it, whereas most Brazilians have great difficulty understanding the European version of their mother tongue.

GETTING BY

In the more popular tourist destinations, most locals speak English, if only at a basic level, and in the Islands and the Algarve, many have a grasp of French and German as well. French was the second language taught in schools up until the 1990s, but since then English has been given greater emphasis. Nowadays the influx of North American popular culture has increased the younger generations' grasp of the English language and, with the growing number of multinational companies in Portugal as well as many people choosing to receive higher education abroad, this tendency promises to continue. None the less, if an effort to speak Portuguese is made, it is greatly appreciated, and any laughing or teasing that may result is certainly not meant to cause offense.

All nouns in Portuguese are either masculine or feminine, and adjectives have a male or female application, with the feminine ending in "a" and the masculine in "o." For example, the feminine noun *flor*, meaning "flower," can be described as *bonita* (pretty), whereas the masculine noun *jardim* (garden) is *bonito*.

Striking the Right Balance

Upon initial contact, the Portuguese can seem distant and aloof, but once a level of trust is established, people let down their guard and readily become friendly. However, you should refrain from using vulgar or coarse language, especially around women, even when relationships have evolved to a more intimate level.

There are three degrees of formality. As in French and Spanish, there are two forms of the second-person singular "you." *Tu* (pronounced "too") is informal, used among peers and people on an intimate standing. The formal *você* (pronounced "vossey"), the equivalent of the French *vous* or Spanish *usted*, is used toward older people and in most professional relationships. In the most formal situations, do not call people "*você*." Use their titles, if they have them (Engineer, Doctor, Architect), or address a male acquaintance as "*senhor*," the equivalent of "sir," or "*Senhor*" followed by his first or last name when these are known (such as *Senhor Luis*, or *Senhor Silva*). Women are called "*minha senhora*" ("madam"), and then "*Dona*" followed by the first name, once known (e.g., *Dona Maria*). The letters *nh* together are pronounced "ni," so that "*senhor*" or "*senhora*" are pronounced "*senior*" and "*seniora.*"

Since the *tu* form and first-name basis are only adopted once a certain level of familiarity is attained, it is best to follow your conversational partner's lead and switch to informal styles only when he or she does. If the other person is significantly older, he or she would adopt the *tu* form with younger people, but would expect to be called "*você*" or "*senhor/a*" by them.

When answering the phone, the Portuguese say "*sim*," or "*estou*" (pronounced "shtow" and meaning "I am here"), or "*está lá*" (pronounced "tah lah" and meaning "is anyone there?"). After saying good-bye, they often say, "*com licença*" (excuse me) before hanging up.

FACE-TO-FACE

The Portuguese are very expressive, and extremely good at face-to-face communication. Their hands and bodies are in constant motion, as if they are trying to illustrate physically what they are saying. Eyebrows, nose, and mouth seem to be moving at all times when they are speaking. With strangers or in unfamiliar situations, people tend to be more discreet, but once they are at ease, conversation and laughter generally become noisy and animated.

TYPICAL GESTURES

The Portuguese use facial expression and body language a lot when they talk, and it is common for someone to actually stand up and move around when telling a story.

Here are some gestures that are typical of Portuguese body language:

- "Let's go": tap the back of the left hand with the right hand.
- In cahoots: rub both forefingers alongside each other.
- If you suspect you've been told a tall tale: pull lower eyelid down, exposing lower eyeball.
- If you are telling a tall tale and want to let someone in on it: wink to that person when your victim isn't looking.
- "Wrap it up": cut-throat signal.
- Appreciative or affirmative: thumbs up.
- To insult a man, use the cuckold sign, raising your forefinger and pinky—but do so at your own peril!

The Portuguese are a very touchy-feely people. They stand close to the person to whom they are talking, and find it natural to touch the other person as they speak. Greetings and farewells between men usually involve many firm hugs and pats on the back, while women tend to grasp each other's arms and hands.

Avoiding eye contact is guaranteed to arouse suspicion, so be sure to look your conversation partner in the eye, and give a firm handshake.

In a crowded place, or if someone is trying to squeeze past you, don't be alarmed or annoyed if they grab your waist or arm and physically move you aside, while saying "*com licença*." Lines are seldom orderly, with people standing very close to the person in front of them and jostling for position.

HUMOR

The Portuguese love a good laugh and are very ready to ridicule others and themselves in the name of fun. For entertainment, they prefer slapstick, or situational comedy that portrays ridiculous and often humiliating situations, rather than a more intellectual or ironic humor. Their literature and *fado* lyrics with humorous intent can often be dark and self-deprecating.

While the Portuguese have a good sense of humor and react well to teasing without too much embarrassment, family members, particularly females, are off-limits. *Alentejanos*, people from the Alentejo, who are generally considered to be slower and lazier than the rest of the population, are the butt of many jokes.

THE MEDIA
Broadcasting

There are four national television networks, two public (RTP1 and RTP2) and two private (Sic and TVI), with the private channels carrying the most sensationalist programming and thereby achieving the highest ratings. All of the channels broadcast international shows and series, generally in the original languages with subtitles. Satellite and cable television is also widely available, providing more than fifty channels of popular national and international broadcasting such as FOX, MTV, BBC World, CNN, Euronews, Eurosport, and Disney.

People listen to the radio mostly in their cars, where morning comedy broadcasts that satirize Portuguese society and politics are a favorite. At home the medium of choice is television, with the most popular programs ranging from *novelas* and talent shows to soccer broadcasts and the news.

Print

Aside from the major international papers, which are available almost everywhere, there are many local newspapers and magazines. The principal daily newspapers (the more conservative *Diário Notícias* in Lisbon and its equivalent in Porto, *Jornal de Notícias*, and the more liberal *Público*) are widely read, as are the main weekend papers,

the *Semanário Económico* and *Expresso,* which are more oriented toward the economy and finance. The two main sports-only newspapers (*Record* and *A Bola*) also command a healthy readership. Popular magazines range from society and gossip publications to fashion and travel titles. Though the Portuguese cultivate a certain conservative restraint in their manner and lifestyle, this attitude contrasts heavily with the graphic depictions of sex and violence in the media. In common with other Mediterranean societies, Portugal is in transition, with the younger generation showing a desire to break away from their parents' and grandparents' traditional values.

Internet

The Portuguese love electronic gadgets. They are avid Internet users and the available technology is modern and ever evolving. Children are encouraged and taught to use computers and the Internet, both at school and at home, and there are numerous easily identifiable cyber cafés in most main towns. Portugal switched to an all-digital broadcasting system in 2012, providing interactive media to a population whose electronic curiosity and adaptability is boundless.

TELEPHONE

Portuguese telecommunications are first-rate, with state-of-the-art technology and services. There are three main providers that offer landlines (MEO, NOS, and Vodafone), and these also provide affordable packages that combine Internet, cable television, and mobile service.

Portugal's country code is 351, and all national phone numbers have nine digits beginning with the number 2. Lisbon's prefix is 21, while Porto numbers begin with 22. In the rest of the country, the first three digits identify the area. All landline telephone services are supplied by Portugal Telecom (PT – whose brand is MEO), which owns most line rentals and supplies to the other providers. Tariffs vary according to the company, but are pretty equal and affordable.

The cell phone craze hit Portugal with a vengeance in the late 1990s. An early advertisement for one of the cell phone operators showed a newborn baby as the only Portuguese citizen who didn't have one! Everyone, including children, has at least one cell phone, and the Portuguese are avid enthusiasts of the latest models and technologies. Like regular telephones, Portuguese cell phone numbers have nine digits, generally beginning with the number 9. As with TV, Internet, and landlines, the three mobile phone operators are MEO, NOS, and Vodafone, and these compete aggressively to dominate this competitive market, offering very reasonable rates and services.

POSTAL SERVICES

The mail service in Portugal is modern and reliable. Portuguese post offices, marked with "CTT" in white letters against a red background, generally operate from 8:30 a.m. to 6:00 p.m. on weekdays, with some open on weekends, but schedules can change depending on the location. Mailboxes can easily be found throughout the cities, with regular mail going in the red boxes and express mail in the blue. Stamps can be purchased at post offices from the service counter or automatic stamp machines as well as many newsstands and bookshops. Since one can do virtually anything at the post office, from paying utility bills to dealing with parking tickets, lines can get quite long. With stamps available in so many other locations and a vast network of ATM machines and Internet solutions that also permit various types of payments, it is usually better to explore other options rather than wait in line at the local CTT office.

CONCLUSION

As you will probably have gathered by now, the Portuguese are as contradictory and confounding as their environment. Older generations who are unwavering in their traditional values and principles live in harmony alongside a young population thirsty for change. While some brood on what could have been and dwell on "*saudade*" for the past, others look to the future with hope, and join in an effort to assert themselves at home and in the world. Historically a daring and courageous people, the Portuguese continue to strive for modernization and self-improvement.

With family at the core of their social life, the Portuguese can at first appear suspicious and even unfriendly toward strangers. This book has sought to offer advice on how to blend in and melt their reticence to reveal a nature that is warm and fun-loving. Join them at the table or participate in their celebrations, and they will teach you how to relax and find pleasure in the simplest things. Explore their cities, seaside towns, and countryside, and you will discover a fascinating, many-layered, and rich history. Portuguese people, once they are assured that your intentions are genuine, will take you under their wing and reward you with loyal and lasting friendship.

Useful Resources

www.moving-on.co
Practical information for foreigners moving to Portugal.

www.visitportugal.com
Official Portuguese tourism website.

www.portugalglobal.pt
General information for tourism and trade.

www.portugal-live.net
Holiday destination guide.

www.portugaltravelguide.com
Detailed travel guide.

www.portugalvirtual.pt
Detailed information for business and pleasure.

www.portugalinbusiness.pt
Promotes Portuguese trade abroad.

www.executiveplanet.com
Guide to international business culture and etiquette.

Transportation
www.cp.pt

Trains
www.carris.pt

Buses (Lisbon)
www.stcp.pt

Buses (Porto)
www.stcp/en/travel

Further Reading

Anderson, Jean. *The Food of Portugal.* New York: William Morrow & Co., 1994.

Barrett, Pam. *Insight Guide, Portugal.* London and New York: APA Publications GmbH & Co. Verlag, 2000.

Birmingham, David. *A Concise History of Portugal.* Cambridge: Cambridge University Press, 2003.

Hole, Abigail, and Charlotte Beech. *Lonely Planet, Portugal.* Melbourne/Oakland/London/Paris: Lonely Planet Publications, 2005.

Jepson, Tim. *Explorer Portugal.* Hampshire: A.A. Publishing, 2001.

Page, Martin. T*he First Global Village: How Portugal Changed the World.* Alfragide: Casa das Letras, 2012 (latest edition. 1st published 2002).

Robertson, Ian. *A Traveller's History of Portugal.* Gloucestershire: The Windrush Press, 2002.

Saraiva, José Hermano. Portugal: *A Companion History (Aspects of Portugal).* Manchester: Carcanet Press Ltd, 1997.

Saramago, Jose. *Journey To Portugal.* London: Vintage. 2002.

Sawday, Alastair. *Special Places to Stay.* Bristol: Alastair Sawday Publishing Co. Ltd., 2003.

Tyson-Ward, Sue. *Living & Working in Portugal.* Oxford: How To Books Ltd., 2002.

Index

acceptance 52
accommodation 136–8
address, forms of
155–6
Afonso Henriques
28–9
Age of Discovery 32–3
agriculture 44
agriturismo 138
air travel 124–5
Alentejo 20, 21, 122
Algarve 20–1, 120, 122
Almeida, Brites de 31
Angola 37, 41, 152
António, Santo 68–9
aparthotels 137
apartments 86, 87, 137
ATMs 92, 116, 162
Azores 12, 13, 15,
33, 153

banks 92, 116–18
baptisms 56, 71–2
Barcelos cockerel 117
bars 87, 93, 114
Beira Interior 17
Beira Litoral 18
birthrate 48–9
body language 156–7
Brazil 33, 36, 121,
152, 153
broadcasting 159
bullfighting 76–9
bureaucracy 99–100
buses 127
business briefing
140–51
business culture 140–3

cable cars 135
Cabo Verde 33, 152
Cabral, Pedro Alvares
33
Caetano, Marcello 41
Carnival 66–7
cars 129–30

Carthaginians 23
Catholicism 56–7
cell phones 161
Celts 22–3
censorship 55
character 8, 9, 48,
51–5, 59–61, 141,
155, 163
cheese 107–8
chicken piri-piri 109
children 48–51, 59–60,
82–3, 90, 92, 93,
96–8
Christianity 25
Christmas 63–4
cinema 122–3
civil war 37
climate 14–15
coffee culture 93–6
Coimbra 10, 18, 74
colonies 37–8, 40–2,
55
communications
152–62
    business 146–8
company structure
and organization
144–5
contracts and
fulfillment 145–6
crime 139
culture 46–7, 122–3
cunhas 142
currency 42, 116

da Gama, Vasco 33
daily life 92–6
dance 66, 122
deadlines 145
decision-making
148–9
desenrascado 141–2
deserts 108–9
Dias, Bartholomeu 33
diet 90
discotheques 114

dolmens 22
Dom Pedro 29
Douro 12, 13, 15, 16,
111, 122
dress code, business
150
driving 128–34
drunk driving 132
Durão Barroso, José
Manuel 46
duty-free goods 124

early inhabitants 21–4
East Timor 152
Easter 64–6
eating out 113–14
economy 43–5
education 98–9
elderly, the 49, 52,
59–60
emigrants 121
English language 84,
154
entertaining, business
150–1
Entre Douro e Minho
15–16
Estado Novo 38–41
estalagens 136–7
Estoril 40, 84, 120
Estremadura e
Ribatejo 18–19, 123
etiquette 84–5
European Union 42,
45, 124
expatriate clubs 83–4
eye contact 158

face-to-face
communications
156–8
fado 72–5
family 48–51, 96, 163
    celebrations 70–2,
    102
Faro 10, 20

Fátima, shrine of 58–9
ferries 128
First Republic 38–9
food 102–9
formality 59–61, 147, 155
Freitas do Amaral, Diogo 46
friends, making 80–5
funerals 56, 72

geography 12–14
gestures 156, 157
gift-giving 82–3
Glass Route 123
global affairs 45–6
Goa 41, 152
golf 120
government 42–3
grandparents 49, 97
Greeks 22
greetings 157–8
guesthouses 138
Guinea 33
Guinea-Bissau 41, 152
Gutteres, António 46

handshakes 59, 146, 158
health 139
    asking about 81, 148
Henry the Navigator 32
history 21–42
homes, Portuguese 86–8
homosexuality 55
hospitals 139
hotels 136–8
household 88–90
houses 86–8
hugs 157
humor 158
hypermarkets 90–1

Iberians 22, 23
identity cards 124
immigration 124
India 33, 40–1
individualism 52–3
industry 44–5, 142–3
Inés de Castro 29
insurance
    medical 139
    motor 132
Internet 160, 162
invitations home 82
Isabel of Aragon 57

Jews 33
João, São 69–70

kings and kingdoms 27–31

labor 143–4
language 152–5
legal system 145–6
leisure time 93, 102–23
life/work balance 141
Lisbon 10, 13, 45, 73, 122
    bridges 127–8
    earthquake (1755) 35–6
    major sites 138
    public transport 134–5
literature 46–7
Lisboa e Setúbal 19
Lusitanians 23–4

Macao 42, 152
machismo 54
Madeira 12, 13, 15, 33, 153
Magalhães, Fernão de 33
magazines 160
manners 8, 59, 81, 84–5

markets 91
marriage 48, 50, 55, 60–1, 70–1
meals 89–90, 102
meat dishes 104–6
media 159–60
metros 134–5
military service 100–1
Minho 12, 15, 16, 122
miracle of the roses 57
Moors 26–9
mortgages 87
Mozambique 37–8, 41, 152
museums 47, 122, 123
music 72–5, 79, 122

Napoleon 36
national pride 53
negotiations 148–9
newspapers 84, 159–60
nightlife 114
nudity 55–6

parking 130–1
Parliament 42–3
pedido 60–1
pensions 137
personal life,
    enquiring about 147–8
pharmacies 91–2
Phoenicians 22
police 139
Pombal, Marquis of 35–6
population 10
Port 111
Porto 10, 13–14, 46, 111, 122
    major sites 138
    public transport 135
Porto Santo 13
postal services 162
pousadas 136

prejudice 55
presentations 148
public holidays 62–3
public transport 134–6
punctuality 92, 144

radio 159
regions 15–21
Rego, Paula 47
religion 10, 50, 56–9
religious holidays 63–6
rental property 86–7
respect 59–61
restaurants 87, 93, 113–14
revolution (1974) 41–2
ribbon-burning 75–6
Romans 24–5
rules of the road 131–3

safety 139
sailing 119–20
saints, popular 67–70
Salazar, António de Oliveira 39–41, 44
São Tomé and Príncipe 33, 152
saudade 61
schools 98
sea food 103–4
second homes 88
Second World War 40
self-catering 137
sexual attitudes 55, 97–8

shopping 90–2, 102
for pleasure 115–16
"Sixty Years' Captivity" 34
smoking 85
soccer 118
sociability 51
soups 106–7
Spain 34
speed limits 133
spies 40
sports 118–21
sports clubs 83
State Tourist Office 138
streetcars 135
suspicion 52, 80

table manners 85
Tagus 12, 13, 19, 127–8
taxis 135–6
teamwork 149–50
telephone 161
television 96, 159
tennis 120
TER (Turismo no Espaço Rural) 138
theater 46
theft 139
time 11
tipico 62
tipping 115
titles 147, 155–6

tolerance 54–5
tolls 133–4
tourism 87
trade unions 143–4
traditions 62
trains 125–7
Trás-os-Montes e Alto Douro 16
travel 124–36

unemployment 50
universities 99
urban regeneration 87

vacations 121–2
Vandals 25
visas 124
Visigoths 25

walking 120–1
water sports 119–20
weather 14–15
weddings 60–1, 70–1
wine 109–13
women
in business 151
in the home 88–9
role of 49, 90
working hours 92, 144–5

youth hostels 137

Acknowledgments

The author would like to thank Nicholas Boothman, Vasco Pinto Basto, and Wendy at talentedwomen.com for their valuable expertise and suggestions.